A Good Read 2

Developing Strategies for Effective Reading

Carlos Islam

Carrie Steenburgh

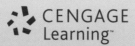

CENGAGE
Learning™

Australia • Brazil • Japan • Korea • Mexico • Singapore • Spain • United Kingdom • United States

A Good Read 2:
Developing Strategies for
Effective Reading
Student Book

Carlos Islam
Carrie Steenburgh

Publishing Director:
Paul Tan

Senior Product Manager:
Michael Cahill

Editor:
Andrew Jessop

Assistant Editor:
Soh Yuan Ting

Senior Publishing Executive:
Gemaine Goh

Illustrator:
Ng Huk Keng

Designer:
Redbean De Pte Ltd

Cover Images:
Getty Images Sales
Singapore Pte Ltd

ISBN-13: 978-981-4246-96-5

ISBN-10: 981-4246-96-4

Cengage Learning Asia Pte Ltd
5 Shenton Way #01-01
UIC Building
Singapore 068808

Cengage Learning is a leading provider of customized learning solutions with office locations around the globe, including Singapore, the United Kingdom, Australia, Mexico, Brazil and Japan.

Locate your local office at: **international.cengage.com/region**

Cengage Learning products are represented in Canada by Nelson Education, Ltd.

For product information, visit **cengageasia.com**

The publisher would like to thank the following for their permission to reproduce photographs on the following pages:

© 2008 Jupiterimages Corporation: 21, 33, 41, 43, 45, 47, 49, 53, 57, 64, 80, 81, 83, 85, 97, 105.
© 2008 Getty Images Sales Singapore Pte Ltd: Cover, 27, 61, 69, 95, 103.

Please note that all people shown are models and are used only for illustrative purposes.

Printed in Singapore
1 2 3 4   11 10 09 08

Dedication and Acknowledgements

We owe a great debt of gratitude to Chris Sol Cruz, Sean Bermingham and Ian Purdon at Cengage Learning. This project owes its life and direction to Chris' initial trust and backing. Sean has steered us through our growing pains while Ian has held our hand nurturing *A Good Read* with his invaluable insights and suggestions.

We thank all the students at Union County College who piloted much of the material in this series and whose feedback has been crucial.

We'd also like to thank our parents for giving us our lives and our characters.

We dedicate this book to Cecelia and Anna.

The publisher would also like to thank the following people for their assistance in developing this series:

Chiou-lan Chern, National Taiwan Normal University
Nancy Garcia, Riverbank High School
Brian Heldenbrand, Jeonju University
Kristin Johannsen
Kevin Knight, Kanda Gaigo Career College
Debra J Martinez
Ahmed M. Motala, University of Sharjah
Tufi Neder Neto, Colégio Loyola
Chris Ruddenklau, Kinki University
Scott Smith, Hongik University
Vilma Sousa, Colégio Rio Branco
Naowarat Tongkam, Silpakorn University
Nobuo Tsuda, Konan University
Cally Williams, Newcomers High School
Young Hee Cheri Lee, Reading Town USA English Language Institute
Zainor Izat Zainal, Universiti Putra Malaysia
Vilma Zapata, Miami-Dade County Public Schools

Contents

Welcome to A Good Read

To the Student:

Reading is a very important part of language learning. Studies show that the more you read, the more you will improve your general English language ability. Through reading, you will build your vocabulary, increase your understanding of grammar, and improve your writing.

In this series, you will find:
- **interesting texts**, on topics such as ambition, life-changing moments, and tough challenges.
- simple explanations of **reading strategies** (ways you can read a text to help understanding), and activities to help you practice these strategies.
- activities to help you recognize and understand word chunks (words that go together, for example, "black and white," "fast car," "spend time") that will help develop your vocabulary.

By practicing reading strategies and learning **word chunks**, you will become a much better reader: You will be able to understand more and enjoy more of what you read.

Carrie and Carlos

To the Teacher:

What do students really need to help them become better readers of English?

A Good Read is designed to help your students become better readers by presenting and practicing **reading strategies** more explicitly and deliberately than other reading series. These strategies range from core reading techniques—such as skimming and scanning, through "guessing" strategies—such as inferring and predicting, to "personal or reflective" strategies—such as visualizing and summarizing. By learning and practicing these strategies, your students will be able to read more naturally, effectively, and fluently.

In addition, Word Work activities accompanying each reading have been included to encourage your students to recognize and understand **word chunks** (groups of words that are frequently found together in texts). Examples of word chunks are "black and white," "leave home," and "first of all." Experts[1] suggest that noticing word chunks improves reading as well as other language skills, as students remember language as whole chunks, not individual words. This saves the reader time and mental energy when reading so that they become more fluent and effective readers.

Carrie and Carlos

---

[1] Lewis, M., 1993, The Lexical Approach, Hove: Language Teaching Publications

Key Features

Start thinking about the unit topic and related language.

Learn how to use the unit's reading strategy.

Try some practice activities.

Read the feedback to check your answers and understanding of the strategy.

Think about the reading and related language.

Complete authentic while reading tasks.

Practice reading strategies covered earlier.

Reflect on the reading and do the activities to check comprehension.

You will read three texts in each unit.

Use the vocabulary index on pages 120—127 to help understand unfamiliar words.

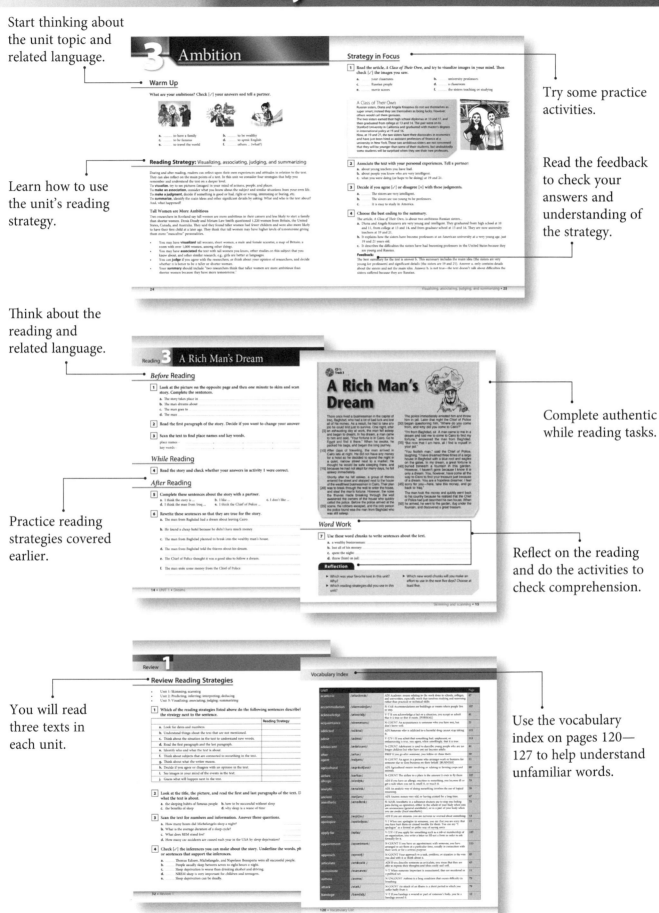

1 Dreams

Warm Up

1 **Read the following statements about dreams. Decide which statement is false.**

   a. In your lifetime, you spend about six years dreaming.
   b. If you are snoring, you cannot be dreaming.
   c. On average, we dream for one or two hours every night, and we usually have four to seven dreams in one night.
   d. Five minutes after the end of the dream, half the dream is forgotten. After 10 minutes, 90 percent is lost.
   e. Men tend to dream more about women, while women dream more about men.
   f. If you are flying in your dream, you are feeling positive about something.

Reading Strategy: Skimming and scanning

BEFORE reading a text carefully, readers can **skim**, or **scan** the text. These strategies help the reader understand what a text is about, and what the main idea is.

To **skim** a text, you read key parts such as headings and look at pictures. You can also just read the first and last sentence of each paragraph. Readers **skim** a text, so they can guess (hypothesize) what the text is about—including its main idea, the type of content the text will cover, the type of language the writer will use, and the attitude of the writer.

To **scan** a text, you look over the text very quickly without stopping or trying to understand the text. You are just looking for the information you need to find: names, places, numbers, dates, or times as well as key words.

Feedback to Warm Up:

Answer: e. Men tend to dream more about other men, while women dream equally about men and women.

Strategy in Focus

1 Read the newspaper headline and the first sentence of the article. Make a hypothesis. What is the article about?

a. A police officer who gets a promotion.
b. A dream that helps a police officer to catch a criminal.
c. A criminal who dreams about a burglary.

NY Detective Solves Crime in her Dream

New York police detective, Captain Maria Gonzalez, arrested a man she had seen in her dreams. The 36-years-old man is charged...

2 Make more hypotheses. What information do you NOT expect to read in the article? Choose one item.

a. A brief description of the detective's dream.
b. A few details about what the man stole.
c. The arrested man's life story.
d. A few details about the arrested man.

3 What words would you expect to read in the article?

a. criminal   b. investigation   c. police   d. your ideas: _____

4 Skim the article (read the first and last sentence of each paragraph). Scan the article for names, places, dates, and numbers. Decide if your hypotheses in the questions above are correct.

New York police detective, Captain Maria Gonzalez, arrested a man she had seen in her dreams. The 36-year-old man is charged with committing a string of burglaries across the city, the police said yesterday. Captain Gonzalez dreamed about the burglaries for three nights. She had been working on the case for several months and was becoming frustrated at the lack of progress. The night before the arrest, Gonzalez saw the face of the criminal in her dream. Gonzalez went to the police station to search the police records. After a few hours, she came across a photo of Cross—the man in her dream—who had been arrested for burglary before.

The arrested man, Julian Cross, 36, has been linked to 10 burglaries dating back to March 4, the police said. The man generally forced his way into apartments, where he stole cash and jewelry.

Feedback:

Your initial hypotheses may not be completely correct. As you skim, scan, and read the article carefully, you should confirm or change your hypotheses. It is important that you make hypotheses to help you understand the text and remember the text better, but your hypotheses will probably change as you read.

Abraham Lincoln's Dream

Before Reading

1 Decide how you should skim a text. Choose the statements you think are correct.
   a. Read the title.
   b. Look at the picture.
   c. Read every word in the text from start to finish.
   d. Read the first paragraph and the last paragraph.
   e. Read the first sentence of each paragraph.
   f. Read the last sentence of each paragraph.
   g. Look at the whole text quickly.

2 Quickly skim the text on the opposite page. What is the text about? Choose one answer. Underline statements that confirm your hypothesis.
   a. Lincoln's dream is that all people are born equal.
   b. Lincoln goes to the funeral of a friend.
   c. Lincoln dreams of his own death.

3 Quickly scan the text to find names, dates, numbers, and pronouns. Answer the following questions.
   a. Was President Lincoln the first president of the USA?
   b. When and where was Lincoln shot?
   c. Who killed Lincoln?

While Reading

4 As you read the text, check your hypothesis in question 2. Underline any statements that confirm your answer.

After Reading

5 Ask a partner the following questions about the text:
   a. Do you think that dreams can predict the future?
   b. Have you ever had a dream that came true?

6 Decide if the statements are true (T) or false (F), according to the text.
   a. T F Abraham Lincoln was the 15th President of the USA.
   b. T F If you dream about death, you probably have a lot of stress in your life.
   c. T F The Civil War was between countries in North and South America.
   d. T F Abraham Lincoln supported the system of slavery.
   e. T F Abraham Lincoln was watching a play when he was shot.

**CD 1:
Track 1**

Abraham Lincoln's Dream

Abraham Lincoln, the 16th President of the United States (1861–1865), is one of the most well known American presidents, not only for his criticism of slavery, but also because he was [5] the first U.S. president to be assassinated. But few people know that Lincoln dreamed about his death a few days before it actually happened.

In his dream, President Lincoln heard people [10] crying, so he got out of bed and went downstairs. Although he could hear them, he could not see anyone. After searching room after room for the cause of this sadness, Lincoln went to the East Room in the White House. There he saw a [15] dreadful sight — a covered corpse and a crowd of people crying over the body. Lincoln demanded to know who had died and was told that the President had been assassinated.

A few days later, on April 14, 1865, Abraham [20] Lincoln was attending a play at the Ford Theater when John Wilkes Booth fired a single shot at Lincoln's head. The President died a day later and his funeral service was held in the East Room of the White House.

[25] Had Lincoln really predicted his own death, or did he just have a dream typical of an important leader? Many believe that this dream was normal for someone who was under severe stress at work. After all, Lincoln was President [30] during the American Civil War when the country's northern and southern states were fighting against each other and many people wanted him dead.

Additionally, dream interpreters believe that if you [35] dream of death, it does not represent your actual death. Instead it probably means that you are under a lot of stress and you want to escape. Certainly this would fit Lincoln's life. Whether he had predicted his own death or just had a typical dream, no one will ever know for sure.

Word Work

7 Complete the sentences with a word chunk from the text. Change the tense if necessary.

a few days before	get out of bed	a crowd of people
have a dream	under a lot of stress	

a. Every morning after the alarm rings, I _____ and take a shower.

b. Last night, I _____ where I was flying with a flock of birds.

c. Because it was the opening night of the movie, there was _____ waiting to buy tickets.

d. High school seniors are _____ because of the university entrance exams.

e. I started studying _____ my English test.

Before Reading

1 Decide how to scan a text. Choose the statement that is NOT correct.

   a. Only look for the information you need.
   b. Look for people's names and place names.
   c. Read the first and last sentence of each paragraph.
   d. Look for dates and numbers.
   e. Look for key words (important words that tell you what the text is about).
   f. Look for proper nouns (words that begin with a capital letter).

2 Take two minutes to skim the text. What is it about? Choose one answer.

   a. A dream the author had about exams.
   b. How dreaming can help you pass exams.
   c. An explanation of why people have exam dreams.

3 Scan the text to find names and key words (words that are repeated and important to the main idea of the text). Which of these are key words are in the text?

   a. _____ dream   **b.** _____ exam   **c.** _____ test
   d. _____ teacher   **e.** _____ bully   **f.** _____ confidence

While Reading

4 As you read the text, check your answer in activity 2. Underline the statements that confirm your answer.

After Reading

5 Ask a partner the following questions:
   a. Have you ever had an exam dream?
   b. Have you ever been in a similar situation to Sang-mi?

6 These are the main ideas for each paragraph. Write the paragraph number next to the statement.

   a. _____ People who have exam dreams are usually successful at work.
   b. _____ Sang-mi's dream is an example of a dream caused by problems.
   c. _____ Everybody has dreams but not everyone remembers them.
   d. _____ People have dreams such as taking an exam because they are worried.
   e. _____ Low confidence can cause people to have exam dreams.

CD 1:
Track 2

Interpreting Exam Dreams

[1] Everyone has several dreams in a night although few people actually remember them. Our dreams usually reflect what is going on in our own lives and they are sometimes about problems we ignore while we are awake.

[2] A friend of mine, Sang-mi, told me about a dream that she has been having since she started her first job after university. In the dream, she sees a classroom in her old high school and there is a group of students taking an exam. There is an empty desk in the room. The exam is nearly finished when she walks into the classroom. As she sits down at the empty desk, the teacher says, "Put your pens down." Then she notices that all the other students are staring at her. As she stands up to leave, she realizes that she is still wearing her pajamas.

[3] When you dream about taking an exam, like Sang-mi, it usually means you are nervous, stressed, or anxious about something. Often in these dreams you cannot answer a test question because it is in a foreign language, or it is about something you have not studied. Other common themes in exam dreams are running out of time, being late, falling asleep, and failing the test.

[4] The reason for having this type of dream has to do with your confidence as well. If your confidence is low, you are more likely to have an exam dream. Something might be happening in your life that makes you feel as though you are being tested, such as a different set of friends, a change of city, or a new job. Sang-mi later told me that she felt she was not prepared for all of her new responsibilities at work. She also thought her colleagues believed she was too inexperienced and not capable in her new position—it was not true, but she didn't have enough confidence in herself.

[5] Despite her anxiety, Sang-mi should not worry too much because people who have exam dreams usually do not fail in life. They usually have very high standards and spend a lot of time on their work. As a result, they usually do very well at whatever they do.

Word Work

7 Correct the mistakes in these word chunks, without looking at the text.

a. I've **nearly closed** my studies and I can't wait to start working and making money.

_____

b. Sometimes, people in exam dreams **run out of hours** and can't finish the test.

_____

c. The night before an exam, I can't **fall to sleep** because I'm so nervous.

_____

d. I have a close **team of friends** and we like to do everything together, including studying for exams.

_____

e. My parents have very **tall standards** for me and expect me to get perfect grades.

_____

Before Reading

1 Look at the picture on the opposite page then take one minute to skim and scan the story. Complete the sentences.

a. The story takes place in _____

b. The man dreams about _____

c. The man goes to _____

d. The man _____

2 Read the first paragraph of the story. Decide if you want to change your answers.

3 Scan the text to find place names and key words.

place names - _____ _____ _____ _____

key words - _____ _____ _____ _____

While Reading

4 Read the story and check whether your answers in activity 1 were correct.

After Reading

5 Complete these sentences about the story with a partner.

a. I think the story is ...   b. I like ...   c. I don't like ...

d. I think the man from Iraq ...   e. I think the Chief of Police ...

6 Rewrite these sentences so that they are true for the story.

a. The man from Baghdad had a dream about leaving Cairo.

_____

b. He found a cheap hotel because he didn't have much money.

_____

c. The man from Baghdad planned to break into the wealthy man's house.

_____

d. The man from Baghdad told the thieves about his dream.

_____

e. The Chief of Police thought it was a good idea to follow a dream.

_____

f. The man stole some money from the Chief of Police.

_____

A Rich Man's Dream

There once lived a businessman in the capital of Iraq, Baghdad, who had a lot of bad luck and lost all of his money. As a result, he had to take any job he could find just to survive. One night, after [5] an exhausting day at work, the man fell asleep and began to dream. In his dream, a man came to him and said, "Your fortune is in Cairo. Go to Egypt and find it there." When he awoke, he packed his bags, and began the long journey.

[10] After days of traveling, the man arrived in Cairo late at night. He did not have any money for a hotel so he decided to spend the night in a quiet, narrow street next to a market. He thought he would be safe sleeping there, and [15] because he had not slept for many days, he fell asleep immediately.

Shortly after he fell asleep, a group of thieves entered the same street and stopped next to the house of the wealthiest businessman in Cairo. [20] Their plan was to break through the wall to enter the house, and steal the man's fortune. However, the noise the thieves made breaking through the wall awakened the owners of the house who quickly called the police. Before the police arrived at the [25] scene, the robbers escaped, and the only person the police found was the man from Baghdad who was still asleep.

The police immediately arrested him and threw him in jail. Later that night the Chief of Police [30] began questioning him, "Where do you come from, and why did you come to Cairo?"

"I'm from Baghdad, sir. A man came to me in a dream and told me to come to Cairo to find my fortune," answered the man from Baghdad. [35] "But now that I am here, all I find is myself in your jail."

"You foolish man," said the Chief of Police, laughing. "I have dreamed three times of a large house in Baghdad with a blue roof and eagles on the gates, In my dream, a great fortune is [40] buried beneath a fountain in this garden. However, I haven't gone because I know it is only a dream. You, however, have come all the way to Cairo to find your treasure just because of a dream. You are a hopeless dreamer. I feel [45] sorry for you—here, take this money, and go back to Iraq."

The man took the money and quickly went back to his country because he realized that the Chief of Police had just described his own house. When [50] he arrived, he went to the garden, dug under the fountain, and discovered a great treasure.

Word Work

7 Use these word chunks to write sentences about the text.

a. a wealthy businessman: _____

b. lost all of his money: _____

c. spent the night: _____

d. threw (him) in jail: _____

Reflection

▶ Which was your favorite text in this unit? Why?
▶ Which reading strategies did you use in this unit?

▶ Which new word chunks will you make an effort to use in the next five days? Choose at least five.

2 Coincidences

Warm Up

Read the coincidences below and rank them from 1 (the biggest coincidence) to 6 (the smallest coincidence).

a. _____ two friends calling each other at exactly the same time

b. _____ finding a friend's lost wallet in the street

c. _____ being on the same flight as a friend

d. _____ two people in a class with the same name

e. _____ two people in a class with the same birthday

f. _____ receiving the same birthday present from two different people

Reading Strategy: Predicting, infering, interpreting, and deducing meaning

WHILE reading, readers can make guesses about what they are reading. This helps improve comprehension and keep interest in the text. In this unit, we look at four types of guesses you can make.

To **make a prediction**, ask yourself, "What will happen next?" or "What word will come next?"

To **make an inference**, ask yourself, "What else do I know about the text that isn't stated?"

To **interpret**, ask yourself "What does the writer mean?"

To **deduce**, ask yourself, "What clues help me guess this difficult word's meaning?"

For example, read the following:

"I was in such a hurry to get to the bank to ask for a mortgage for our dream house that I forgot to put on a tie. Luckily, I ran into a friend outside the bank who …"

- You can **predict** that the friend gave the writer a tie.
- You can **infer** that the writer was late for the meeting because he was in a hurry.
- You can **interpret** that the writer met a friend by accident outside the bank and did not physically run into the friend.
- You can **deduce** from the context that a mortgage is a loan to buy a house.

Strategy in Focus

1 Read the first sentence of the text and predict the last word.

> ## Coincidence on a Train
> In 1922, three Englishmen were traveling separately by train through ...

Feedback:

"Peru" is the word the writer uses, but other predictions would be any country or place, such as Spain, Tokyo, a tunnel, or the countryside.

2 Continue reading Coincidence on a Train. Then check [✓] the inferences you can make.

a. _____ The men were wealthy.　　**b.** _____ The three men did not like each other.
c. _____ The men had never met before.　　**d.** _____ It was not an electric train.

> In 1922, three Englishmen were traveling through Peru. At the time of their introduction, they were the only three men in the railroad car. Their introductions were more surprising than they could have imagined. One man said his last name was Bingham, and the second man said his last name was Powell. The third man announced that his last name was Bingham-Powell. None of the men were related in any way. The men were left speechless by the coincidence.

Feedback:

We can infer that the men were wealthy because foreign travel was very expensive in the 1920s (a.); the men had never met before because they introduced themselves to each other (c.); electric trains were not common until the 1960s (d.).

3 Interpret what the writer means by "The men were left speechless by the coincidence."

a. The men were not able to speak.
b. The men were very surprised.

Feedback:

The correct answer is b. The men were so surprised that they didn't know what to say.

4 Deduce the meaning of "announced" in the sentence, "The third man announced that his last name was Bingham-Powell."

a. Said to the other men.
b. Shouted at the other men.
c. Wrote to the other men.

Feedback:

The correct answer is a. The men are simply telling each other their names.

A Whale of a Time

Before Reading

1 Look at the title of the news story and the picture. What do you think the story is about? Choose one answer.

a. A family that has an accident with a whale.
b. A place you can see a lot of whales.
c. A whale that can tell the time.

2 Read the beginning of the text. Predict what happens next. Choose one answer.

The Johnson family, from Coventry in England, believe they are lucky to be alive after surviving an incredible incident off the coast of Australia. The Johnsons had been told that they might see some whales when they were chartering a yacht for a 10-day sailing trip around the Whitsunday Islands. However, they had no clue just how close their viewing would be.

a. A whale hit their boat.
b. The Johnson family got lost.
c. The Johnson family caught a whale.

While Reading

3 As you read the text, check your hypothesis and your prediction. Decide if you want to change your answers.

After Reading

4 Check [✓] the inferences you can make about the text.

a. _____ The Johnson family has more than one son.
b. _____ The whale thought the yacht was another whale.
c. _____ It is very unusual for whales to have accidents with boats.
d. _____ The whale was angry that the Johnson family was close to its baby.
e. _____ The whale hit the mast of the Johnson's yacht.

5 Find the underlined words in the text. Deduce the meaning from the context. Then circle the synonyms.

a. They were <u>chartering</u> a yacht for a 10-day sail. renting / sailing
b. A humpback whale <u>leapt</u> out of the ocean. swam / jumped
c. The yacht had <u>inadvertently</u> sailed between the whale and its baby calf. accidentally / strangely
d. The chance of it happening is <u>miniscule</u>. very small / very good

A Whale of a Time

The Johnson family, from Coventry in England, believe they are lucky to be alive after surviving an incredible incident off the coast of Australia. The Johnsons had been told that they might see
[5] some whales when they were chartering a yacht for a 10-day sailing trip around the Whitsunday Islands. However, they had no clue just how close their viewing would be. Two hours into their journey a nine-meter-long humpback whale
[10] leapt out of the ocean and crashed into their boat before returning to the water.

Mark Johnson, the eldest son, was sailing the yacht when he heard an immense bang and a thud. He immediately thought the yacht had hit
[15] a rock. However, when he looked up, he saw the whale sliding down the deck of the boat. He told reporters, "We were staring into its right eye. It was a very scary moment. The eye was about the size of a dinner plate. It was huge."

[20] Luckily for the Johnson family, no one was hurt, but the yacht suffered severe damage. The whale had ruined the mast and rigging—the pole and ropes which hold the sail—and so the family was stranded at sea, 10 miles from the shore.
[25] The radio equipment was also damaged, but fortunately they had a cell phone and were able
[30] to call for help. About one and a half hours later, another boat arrived to take them back to shore.

Why the whale jumped onto the yacht is a
[35] mystery, but the family thinks that maybe the boat had inadvertently sailed between the whale and its baby calf. Perhaps the whale was trying to reach its calf when it jumped, and hit the yacht by chance.

[40] Whatever the reason, people are completely amazed that this incident happened. There is over 135 million square miles of ocean, so what are the chances of a whale jumping onto a 30-foot-long yacht? The chance of something like
[45] this happening is miniscule, but it just shows that life is full of surprises.

Word Work

6 Rewrite the sentences using these word chunks. Change the tense if necessary.

| off the coast of | have no clue | leap out of | call for help | by chance |

a. **Luckily**, I had reviewed my science notes so I was prepared for the surprise quiz.

b. When I realized I had overslept on my first day of work, I **jumped out of** bed, quickly put on my clothes, and ran out the door.

c. I **have no idea** what I want to do when I graduate from college.

d. I love sailing and my dream is to someday charter a yacht and sail it **along the shore of** Mexico.

e. After my car broke down on the interstate, I used my cell to **phone for assistance**.

Before Reading

1 Quickly skim the text. Read the title as well as the first and last sentence of each paragraph. What is the text about?

a. Coincidences do not happen.

b. Most coincidences are quite common.

c. Most coincidences are magical because they are so strange.

While Reading

2 As you read the text, decide if you want to change your hypothesis.

After Reading

3 Decide if you agree [✓] or disagree [×] with the interpretations of these sentences.

	Interpretation	✓ / ×
a. "We think something like that has to be more than chance." (line 7)	It is something magical or mysterious—not mathematical or logical.	
b. "Mathematicians say that even in the most unbelievable situations, the probabilities are actually quite high." (line 10)	Coincidences happen a lot more than people think.	
c. "And that is the beauty of coincidences; they just seem to magically occur." (line 45)	Coincidences are interesting to people because it seems like something mysterious is happening.	
d. "mathematical explanations are not as mysterious and exciting as the belief that some things happen by magic." (line 49)	People think mathematics is boring.	

4 Choose the best definition of the word in bold. Look at the surrounding words to help you deduce the meaning.

a. "When such coincidental **occurrences** happen, we're amazed." (line 6)

   i.   something that happens   **ii.** someone who can do magic

b. "Using probability theory, mathematicians can **figure out** the odds of something happening." (line 15)

   i.   calculate   **ii.** draw

c. "In order to **guarantee** that two people share the same birthday, you would need to ... "(line 20)

   i.   remember   **ii.** be 100 percent sure

Coincidence? Probably Not

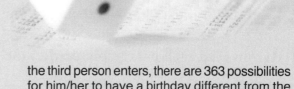

We have all experienced some sort of coincidence, whether it is a friend calling just as we are about to call them, or running into an old friend or acquaintance while traveling, [5] or sharing the same birthday as a friend. When such coincidental occurrences happen, we are amazed. We think something like that has to be more than chance. But do such events really happen by chance?

[10] Mathematicians say that even in the most unbelievable situations, the probabilities are actually quite high. In a big wide world, "coincidences" happen all the time.

Using probability theory, mathematicians can [15] figure out the odds of something happening. For example, let's say you want to figure out the odds of two classmates sharing the same birthday. Mathematicians have created a "birthday problem" formula to calculate this. In [20] order to guarantee that two people share the same birthday, you would need to gather together 366 people (i.e. one more person than the total number of days in a year). However, if you are willing to accept a 50/50 chance, you [25] only need 23 people. So how did mathematicians come up with this surprisingly small number?

Imagine the students entering the room one by one. When the second person enters the room, there are 364 possible days for him/her to have [30] a birthday different from the first person. When the third person enters, there are 363 possibilities for him/her to have a birthday different from the previous two. This can be expressed mathematically as 364/365 x 363/365. [35] Continuing in this way, when 23 people are in the room, the probability of everyone having a different birthday is 364/365 x 363/365 x 362/365 x ... x 343/365 = 0.492. Thus, the probability that at least two of the 23 students have the [40] same birthday is 1 - 0.492 = 0.508, i.e. a 50/50 chance.

Most people do not usually ask the birthday of everybody they meet. If they did, they would discover that many people share the same [45] birthday. And that is the beauty of coincidences; they just seem to magically occur.

While probability theory can explain the chances of something happening, many people ignore this explanation. After all, mathematical explanations [50] are not as mysterious and exciting as the belief that some things happen by magic.

Word Work

5 Make word chunks from the text using these words.

run	let's	willing	come	one

a. _____ up with
b. _____ say
c. _____ into (someone)
d. _____ by one
e. _____ to accept

Before Reading

1 Look at the pictures below and guess what the story is about.

  a. Two friends who meet coincidentally.
  b. A young girl who helps old people.
  c. An old lady who loses an expensive scarf.

While Reading

2 Read the first paragraph and check your hypothesis.

3 As you read each paragraph, predict the picture for the next paragraph.

A _____   B _____   C _____

D _____   E _____   F _____

After Reading

4 Ask a partner these questions:

  a. What were the coincidences in the story?
  b. Do you know of similar or bigger coincidences?

5 Check [✓] the inferences you can make about the story. Underline the words, phrases, or sentences that support them.

  a. _____ It was dangerous in Hungary during the Second World War.
  b. _____ Kathy and Monica didn't say "goodbye" to each other before leaving Hungary.
  c. _____ Eliza didn't live with her parents.
  d. _____ Eliza thinks she will get the job.
  e. _____ Monica and Kathy spent their adult lives living in the same city.
  f. _____ Monica and Kathy didn't recognize each other.

The Lucky Silk Scarf

Kathy could clearly remember the night she had to leave her home in Hungary. It was the beginning of the Second World War and her family needed to escape as soon as possible.
[5] She quickly packed a suitcase with a few pieces of clothing, her diary, and her most prized possession, a beautiful silk scarf. Kathy and her best friend, Monica, had persuaded their parents to buy them matching scarves, which
[10] they each wore tied around their neck as a symbol of their friendship. Kathy had no idea that she was going to America that night and would not be returning.

Kathy kept that special silk scarf for many years.
[15] One day she decided to give it to her granddaughter, Eliza, to wear to her first job interview for good luck. Kathy was afraid that Eliza would lose the scarf, but her granddaughter reassured her, "Don't worry, Grandma, nothing's
[20] going to happen to your scarf. You'll see. It is going to bring both of us luck today." And with that, Eliza kissed her grandmother on the cheek and left for the interview.

That afternoon, Eliza left the interview feeling
[25] confident that she had got the job so she decided to celebrate by going to a restaurant.

As she was sitting at her table, she felt someone staring at her. Sitting next to her was an elderly
[30] woman who could not take her eyes off her. "I'm sorry, do I know you?" Eliza asked.

"I'm sorry, dear, but you remind me of someone I once knew," the old woman replied. "My best friend looked like you and used to wear a scarf
[35] just like the one you're wearing around your neck." Eliza felt goose bumps travel up her arm. She had heard stories of her grandmother's best friend and knew the significance of the scarf. Could this be Monica, her grandmother's
[40] childhood friend?

Eliza introduced herself and waited to hear the name of the other woman. "My name's Monica, dear. I'm originally from Hungary, but my family had to leave when I was fourteen and I've been
[45] living here in California ever since." Eliza could not believe it. She said, "Monica, would you mind coming somewhere with me? I need to show you something." The older woman agreed and they left the restaurant together.

[50] They walked the short distance to Kathy's home and rang the door bell. When Kathy opened the door, she was amazed to see her childhood friend standing in front of her. The scarf had indeed brought good luck.

Word Work

6 Circle the correct word chunk.

a. I **clearly remember / plainly remember** the day I got accepted into the university.

b. My mother's engagement ring is her most **prized possession / award possession**.

c. My first **work interview / job interview** was at a well-known bank.

d. Everyone says that I **look like / resemble like** my mother.

Reflection

▶ Which was your favorite text in this unit? Why?

▶ Which reading strategies did you use in this unit?

▶ Which new word chunks will you make an effort to use in the next five days? Choose at least five.

3 Ambition

Warm Up

What are your ambitions? Check [✓] your answers and tell a partner.

a. _____ To have a family.　　　**b.** _____ To be wealthy.
c. _____ To be famous.　　　　 **d.** _____ To speak English.
e. _____ To travel the world.　　**f.** Other: _____

Reading Strategy: Visualizing, associating, judging, and summarizing

During and after reading, readers can reflect upon their own experiences and attitudes in relation to the text. They can also reflect on the main points of a text. In this unit we consider four strategies that help you remember and understand the text on a deeper level.

To **visualize**, try to see pictures (images) in your mind of actions, people, and places.

To **make an association**, consider what you know about the subject and similar situations from your own life.

To **make a judgment**, decide if something is good or bad, right or wrong, interesting or boring, etc.

To **summarize**, identify the main ideas and other significant details by asking: What and who is the text about? And, what happened?

Tall Women are More Ambitious

Two researchers in Scotland say tall women are more ambitious in their careers and less likely to start a family than shorter women. Denis Deady and Miriam Law-Smith questioned 1,220 women from Britain, the United States, Canada, and Australia. They said they found taller women had fewer children and were also more likely to have their first child at a later age. They think that tall women may have higher levels of testosterone, giving them more "masculine" personalities.

- You may have **visualized** tall women, short women, a male and female scientist, a map of Britain, a room with over 1,000 women, among other things.
- You may have **associated** the text with tall women you know, other studies on this subject that you know about, and other similar research, e.g., girls are better at languages.
- You can **judge** if you agree with the researchers, or think about your opinion of researchers, and decide whether it is better to be a taller or shorter woman.
- Your **summary** should include "two researchers think that taller women are more ambitious than shorter women because they have more testosterone."

Strategy in Focus

1 Read the article, *A Class of Their Own*, and try to visualize images in your mind. Then check [✓] the images you saw.

a. _____ your classmates

b. _____ university professors

c. _____ Russian people

d. _____ a classroom

e. _____ movie scenes

f. _____ the sisters teaching or studying

A Class of Their Own

Russian sisters, Diana and Angela Kniazeva do not see themselves as super smart; instead they see themselves as being lucky. However, others would call them geniuses.

The two sisters earned their high school diplomas at 10 and 11, and then graduated from college at 13 and 14. The pair went on to Stanford University in California and graduated with master's degrees in international policy at 15 and 16.

Now, at 19 and 21, the two sisters have their doctorates in economics and have just been hired as assistant professors of finance at a university in New York. These two ambitious sisters are not concerned that they will be younger than some of their students, but undoubtedly some students will be surprised when they see their new professors.

2 Associate the text with your personal experiences. Tell a partner:

a. about young teachers you have had.

b. about people you know who are very intelligent.

c. what you were doing (or hope to be doing) at 19 and 21.

3 Decide if you agree [✓] or disagree [×] with these judgments.

a. _____ The sisters are very intelligent.

b. _____ The sisters are too young to be professors.

c. _____ It is easy to study in America.

4 Choose the best ending to the summary.

The article, *A Class of Their Own*, is about two ambitious Russian sisters...

a. Diana and Angela Kniazeva are very young and intelligent. They graduated from high school at 10 and 11, from college at 13 and 14, and from graduate school at 15 and 16. They are now university teachers at 19 and 21.

b. It explains how the sisters have become professors at an American university at a very young age, just 19 and 21 years old.

c. It describes the difficulties the sisters have had becoming professors in the United States because they are young and Russian.

Feedback:

The best summary for the text is answer b. This summary includes the main idea (the sisters are very young for professors) and significant details (the sisters are 19 and 21). Answer a. only contains details about the sisters and not the main idea. Answer c. is not true—the text doesn't talk about difficulties the sisters suffered because they are Russian.

The Pursuit of Happyness is Pure Pleasure

Before Reading

1 Skim the movie review. Answer the questions.

a. Is it a positive review?   **b.** Is the movie a comedy?   **c.** Have you seen the movie?

While Reading

2 Read the review and decide if you want to see the movie. If you have already seen the movie, confirm your answers to question 1a and 1b.

After Reading

3 Decide if you agree [✓] or disagree [×] with these judgments.

a. _____ The movie seems interesting.

b. _____ The story isn't realistic.

c. _____ Will Smith is a great actor.

4 Circle the images you visualized in your mind. Describe them and any others you saw to a partner.

children you know	scenes from a movie	homeless people
your father	people in an office	images of San Francisco

5 Associate the text with your personal experiences and answer these questions.

a. Have you seen similar movies (e.g. based on true stories)?

b. Can you describe a situation where you were desperate?

c. What was your life like when you were five years old?

6 Choose the best ending to the summary.

The Pursuit of Happyness is Pure Pleasure is a positive review of the 2006 Will Smith movie...

a. The review praises Smith for his performance in the real life story of Chris Gardner. Gardner raises his son alone in very difficult circumstances including homelessness. He wants to have a successful career as a stockbroker and support his son, but has to suffer before reaching his dream.

b. The review explains how Smith plays a father of a five-year-old boy who is trying to get a good job. He leaves his job as a salesman to take an important internship. He wants to give his son a good future and takes a chance. Although Gardner is very intelligent and hard working, he finds it very hard because he doesn't have anywhere to live and gets into a lot of debt.

CD 1:
Track 7

The Pursuit of Happyness is Pure Pleasure

Directed by Gabriele Muccino

Will Smith's movie characters have fought aliens in *Men in Black,* crime in *Bad Boys* and boxers in *Ali.* In *The Pursuit of Happyness*, Smith plays the role of a man who has to fight poverty.

[5] This movie is based on the true life story of 30-year-old Chris Gardner, a struggling salesman who is running short of money but is full of ambition. Set in San Francisco in 1981, Gardner is stuck in a dead-end job, and knows

[10] that if he wants to give his five-year-old son, Christopher (played by Smith's actual son, Jaden Christopher Syre Smith in his debut role) a better future, he needs to make some changes in his life. Gardner talks his way into an important

[15] internship at a top stockbroker's firm, but it is a risky move. It is an unpaid position and there is little chance that he'll be offered a paying job at the end of it.

Gardner is an intelligent, successful intern by

[20] day, and a desperate, homeless father living in a train station at night. The movie is emotionally exhausting as you see this hard-working, loving father become more and more desperate and in debt. To make matters worse, he is left to

[25] raise his son alone after Christopher's mother leaves them to live in New York. All he wants to do is protect his son but being a single father is difficult, and being broke only makes it worse. The script is excellent; but even without dialog,

[30] Smith's expressions capture the panic of a father who is afraid of failing and of losing his son.

Throughout the movie, you are hoping Gardner will succeed, and his positive attitude in the face of such difficulties is truly inspiring. Even though

[35] the movie is based on a true story, some critics have said that *The Pursuit of Happyness* does not reflect reality because Gardner never seems to tire or lose hope in his dream to be successful even when he is homeless. Despite this criticism,

[40] the ending leaves you with a warm feeling and Smith does an excellent job of making us believe that anything is possible if you put your mind to it.

Word Work

7 Match the word chunk with its synonym. Then choose one word chunk and write a sentence about yourself or someone you know.

- **a.** run short of money •
- **b.** a dead-end job •
- **c.** a risky move •
- **d.** put your mind to it •
- **e.** a warm feeling •

- **• i.** a good sensation
- **• ii.** do something dangerous
- **• iii.** have very little finances
- **• iv.** no possibility of promotion
- **• v.** try very hard to do something

From Refugee to Harvard Graduate

Before Reading

1 What words do you associate with refugees? Write down words you think could appear in the text.

_____   _____   _____   _____

_____   _____   _____   _____

While Reading

2 As you read the text, visualize images in your mind.

After Reading

3 Check [✓] any of these images you saw while reading the story. Describe them and any others you saw to a partner.

a. _____ A map of Africa.   **b.** _____ People walking across a desert.

c. _____ A camp full of people.   **d.** _____ People flying to the USA.

e. _____ Mawi studying at university.   **f.** _____ A graduation ceremony.

4 Decide if you agree [✓] or disagree [×] with these judgments.

Paragraph 2:

a. _____ Mawi and his family were lucky to survive the desert.

b. _____ It must be horrible to live in a refugee camp for three years.

Paragraph 3:

a. _____ Mawi's parents must have strong personalities.

b. _____ Mawi's father was lucky to get a job in America.

Paragraph 4:

a. _____ Mawi must be angry at people who drink and drive.

b. _____ Mawi must be very intelligent to go to Harvard.

Paragraph 5:

a. _____ Mawi is a very generous and kind person.

b. _____ I would like to meet Mawi.

5 Choose two statements that best complete a summary.

The text is about Mawi, an Ethiopian refugee who has had a very successful life in America...

a. His family spent years of hardship first surviving a refugee camp in the Sudan and then struggling to make a living in Chicago.

b. Mawi and his family left Ethiopia when he was four years old and his father got a job as a doctor.

c. Despite his family struggling to make a living and suffering personal tragedy, Mawi went to Harvard and now has a successful career.

From Refugee to Harvard Graduate

[1] In 1980, there was a civil war in the East African country, Ethiopia. Rebel groups forced thousands of Ethiopians to leave their villages. Many escaped to refugee camps in Sudan. The journey was difficult and dangerous, especially for young children. There was an immense desert to cross and refugees also had to avoid rebel groups and people involved in slavery.

[2] Mawi Asgedom and his family were among those families forced to leave their village. Mawi was only four at the time. The family walked hundreds of miles across the desert to a Sudanese refugee camp. They lived there for three years before they were able to move to the United States. They arrived in Chicago, without much money, without much English, but with plenty of ambition. They were determined to stay together and succeed in their new home.

[3] Mawi's father, once a respected doctor, became a janitor because no other work was available. It was not the job he wanted and it was not well paid, but it put food on the table. Both parents were determined their children would have a better life than they had had. As Mawi wrote in a book about his life, *Of Beetles and Angels*, "They told us that we could do anything if we worked hard and treated people with respect."

[4] Mawi adapted to the new culture, learned English and, despite some terrible difficulties including the death of his elder brother, he succeeded in high school and received a full scholarship to Harvard. During his junior year at college, his father was killed by a drunk driver, just as his brother had been killed five years earlier.

[5] Many people would have gotten depressed and given up at that point, but not Mawi. Instead, he decided to work even harder and dedicate his entire life to making other people's lives better. In his book he describes his experiences from living in a refugee camp to going on to successfully graduate from Harvard. He started a foundation in memory of his father and brother. The foundation provides educational support to recently arrived third world immigrants in the USA. He is also a motivational speaker, working with teenagers, spreading his message that with ambition and hard work, dreams can become reality.

Word Work

6 Match the words to make word chunks from the text. Then choose one word chunk and write a sentence about yourself or someone you know.

a. put •

b. treat •

c. adapt •

d. receive •

e. spread •

• i. (someone's) message

• ii. people with respect

• iii. to a new culture

• iv. bread on the table

• v. a full scholarship

Before Reading

1 Write down words you think could appear in the story, The Tiny Samurai.

_____   _____   _____   _____

_____   _____   _____   _____

While Reading

2 As you read the text, try to visualize images in your mind.

After Reading

3 Tell a partner about the images you saw.

4 What associations did you make while you were reading? Check [✓] or cross [×] the ideas you had.

Paragraph	Association	Yes / No
1.	**a.** Things you know about ancient Japan, e.g. clothes, samurai.	
	b. How to feed and clothe a one-inch baby.	
2.	**a.** Things you have seen or read about samurai.	
	b. A time your parents have helped you do something.	
3.	**a.** When you have made new friends.	
	b. How Issun Boshi sounded, e.g. did he have a high voice?	
4.	**a.** Someone you have protected.	
	b. A story you know about a brave person protecting someone.	
5.	**a.** A time your dreams came true.	
	b. A time you had to fight someone.	

5 Read the summaries and decide which one is the best.

a. The Tiny Samurai is about a small Japanese boy who dreams about being a samurai. His parents helped him travel to Kyoto in a rice bowl. After going to Kyoto and demonstrating his courage, he achieved his ambitions.

b. The Tiny Samurai is about a very small boy called Issun Boshi. He was only one inch tall, but he wanted to be a samurai. One day Issun Boshi saved his friend Haruhime from a demon. They used the demon's magic hammer to make Issun Boshi taller and he became a samurai.

c. The Tiny Samurai is about a Japanese boy who travels to Kyoto to train to be a samurai. He meets a Lord who helps him achieve his dream.

The Tiny Samurai

[1] Once upon a time, there was a kind old couple who desperately wanted a child. They prayed and prayed until finally their wish came true and a baby was born. The boy was healthy and normal in every way except for his size: he was only about one inch tall. His parents called him Issun-Boshi.

[2] Although most babies grow, Issun-Boshi remained the same size, but this did not stop him from having big dreams. He dreamed of traveling down the river to the old capital city of Kyoto to become a Japanese warrior—a brave samurai. His parents did not want him to leave, but they realized they could not stop him, so they helped him prepare for his big trip. They gave him a rice bowl which he used as a boat, chopsticks to use as paddles, and a needle which he could use as a sword to protect himself.

[3] The trip to Kyoto was dangerous. The river was full of rocks and it had fast-moving water, but Issun-Boshi was brave and strong. He was determined to become a samurai. When he finally arrived in Kyoto, he went to the grandest house to ask for a job. The lord of the house was impressed by Issun-Boshi's courage and gave him a job. He allowed his beautiful daughter Haruhime to play with Issun-Boshi. Over the years Issun-Boshi and Haruhime became best friends.

[4] One spring day Haruhime wanted to visit a temple. It was a dangerous walk because there were demons around who would kidnap young women, so her father ordered some of his strongest warriors to go with her. As usual, Issun-Boshi also joined her. As they were walking, a demon appeared in the middle of the road. Instead of protecting Haruhime, all the warriors ran away. Issun-Boshi bravely stood up to the demon, but he was soon swallowed by the hideous monster in one gulp. The demon was about to kidnap Haruhime when he felt an incredible pain. It was Issun Boshi stabbing him with a needle. It was so painful that the demon quickly spat Issun-Boshi out of his mouth and ran away.

[5] After the demon left, Haruhime noticed that he had left a magic hammer. She knew that it would grant any wish, so she asked her hero what he wanted. Issun-Boshi replied that he wanted to be bigger, so Haruhime took the hammer, pointed it at him, and he grew to be six feet (1.8m) tall. This is how Issun-Boshi became one of the most respected samurais in Kyoto.

Word Work

6 Spot the difference. Underline any word chuncks that are different from the original text. There are six differences.

A very long time ago, there was a nice elderly couple who desperately wanted a child. They prayed and prayed, until finally their prayers were answered and they had a child. The boy was healthy and normal in every way apart from his size: he only stood at about one inch high. His parents called him Issun Boshi.

Reflection

▶ Which was your favorite text in this unit? Why?

▶ Which reading strategies did you use in this unit?

▶ Which new word chunks will you make an effort to use in the next five days? Choose at least five.

Review Reading Strategies

- Unit 1: Skimming; scanning
- Unit 2: Predicting; inferring; interpreting; deducing
- Unit 3: Visualizing; associating; judging; summarizing

1 Which of the reading strategies listed above do the following sentences describe? Write the strategy next to the sentence.

	Reading Strategy
a. Look for dates and numbers.	
b. Understand things about the text that are not mentioned.	
c. Think about the situation in the text to understand new words.	
d. Read the first and last paragraphs.	
e. Identify who and what the text is about.	
f. Think about subjects that are connected to something in the text.	
g. Think about what the writer means.	
h. Decide if you agree or disagree with an opinion in the text.	
i. See images in your mind of the events in the text.	
j. Guess what will happen next in the text.	

2 Look at the title and the picture then read the first and last paragraphs of the text. Decide what the text is about.

a. The sleeping habits of famous people.　　**b.** How to be successful without sleep.
c. The benefits of sleep.　　**d.** Why sleep is a waste of time.

3 Scan the text for numbers and information. Answer these questions.

a. How many hours did Michelangelo sleep a night? _____

b. What is the average duration of a sleep cycle? _____

c. What does REM stand for? _____

d. How many car accidents are caused each year in the USA by sleep deprivation? _____

4 Check [✓] the inferences you can make about the story. Underline the words, phrases, or sentences that support the inferences.

a. _____ Thomas Edison, Michelangelo, and Napoleon Bonaparte were all successful people.
b. _____ People usually sleep between seven to eight hours a night.
c. _____ Sleep deprivation is worse than drinking alcohol and driving.
d. _____ NREM sleep is very important for children and teenagers.
e. _____ Sleep deprivation can be deadly.

Reading

CD 1:
Track 10

The Importance of Sleep

Michelangelo, Napoleon Bonaparte, Thomas Edison, Donald Trump, and Madonna all have something in **common**—they have all claimed to only need four hour's sleep a night. Does this
[5] prove that the **key** to success is to sleep less? On the **contrary**, most people need much more sleep to keep healthy, regulate their emotions, and strengthen cognitive skills such as memory. What actually happens during sleep that
[10] recharges our body and makes us healthy?

A sleep cycle, which usually takes about 90—110 minutes, is divided into two phases, non-rapid eye movement (NREM) and rapid eye movement (REM). During the first stage of
[15] NREM, which is drowsiness, our muscle activity slows down, but we are still not fully asleep. After ten minutes of this drowsiness, our bodies enter the second stage of NREM, light sleep, which lasts about twenty minutes. Our breathing
[20] and heart rate slow down and then we enter deep sleep, stages three and four. These are the most restorative stages. Our blood pressure drops, growth and development hormones are released, and energy is regained. We then enter

[25] the second phase of the sleep cycle, REM sleep, which is when our brain is most active and the majority of dreams occur. Scientists believe that dreaming allows the processing and retention of memories. This phase usually lasts about
[30] ten minutes and then the cycle is repeated. A person may go through four or five sleep cycles a night.

Sleep deprivation, not getting enough sleep, has a number of negative consequences.
[35] Besides feeling tired and moody, drowsy people usually have more difficulty remembering facts, concentrating on tasks, and reacting to situations. For example, in the USA alone, more than 56,000 car accidents a year, some fatal, are
[40] caused by drivers feeling sleepy **behind** the wheel. In fact, studies show that sleepy drivers are impaired at a level equal to that of drivers who have drunk alcohol.

So, although Thomas Edison regarded sleep as
[45] a **waste** of time, most people do need more than just a few hours of sleep a night. It is the easiest way to become a smarter and healthier person.

Comprehension Check

1 Decide if the statements are true (T) or false (F), according to the article.

a. T F The sleep cycle is composed of two phases, NREM and REM.

b. T F A person usually has three to four sleep cycles a night.

c. T F Light sleep is the most restorative stage of NREM.

d. T F Thomas Edison thought sleep was important for his health.

2 The word "drowsy" in the passage is closest in meaning to:

a. unhappy   b. forgetful   c. sleepy   d. upset

3 Which of the following is NOT mentioned in the text as a benefit of sleeping?

a. blood pressure decreases   b. improved memory
c. more energy   d. better relationships

4 The word "restorative" in the passage is closest in meaning to:

a. damaging   b. restful   c. healing   d. tiring

5 Choose three sentences that best complete a summary of the text.

Getting enough sleep is important for being healthy, happy, and intelligent...

a. Sleep deprivation can result in moodiness, tiredness, and even death.

b. The singer, Madonna, only sleeps four hours a night.

c. People usually have four to five sleep cycles a night.

d. During NREM sleep, blood pressure is regulated, and growth and development hormones are released.

e. Most car accidents are caused by driving while tired.

f. REM sleep is important for improving memory and thinking skills.

More Word Chunks

1 Match the word chunk with its definition. Then choose one word chunk and write a sentence about yourself or someone you know.

a. have something in common •   • i.   in contrast
b. the key to success •   • ii.   while driving
c. on the contrary •   • iii. worthless or useless activity
d. behind the wheel •   • iv.   the most important factor
e. a waste of time •   • v.   share a similar trait or characteristic

2 Complete the sentences using the following word chunks from Units 1, 2, and 3.

bed	asleep	time	stress
move	job	money	

a. Lately, I have had trouble **falling** _____ when I go to bed.

b. I am **under a lot of** _____ at work and instead of sleeping I think about all the work I have to do.

c. Sometimes it helps if **I get out of** _____ and write down my thoughts in a journal.

d. I want to quit my **dead-end** _____ but I am afraid that I will **run short of** _____ and won't be able to pay my bills.

e. I know it's a **risky** _____ but I hope to start my own business some day.

f. I'd like to have my own business before I'm 35. I'm 33 now so I need to be making plans before I run out of _____.

---

3 In Units 1 and 3, we learned to use the word chunks "run out of time" and "once upon a time."

> The English exam was too long and I couldn't complete it because **I ran out of time**.
> **Once upon a time** is a popular start to fairy tales.

word chunk	definition
from time to time	sometimes
in no time	very quickly
kill time	to do something while waiting
before your time	before you were alive
to lose time	to take longer
about time	something should have happened a while ago
take your time	do not hurry

Complete the following sentences with a "time" word chunk from above. Change the verb tense and pronoun when necessary.

a. Whenever I take a math test, I like to _____ so I don't make any foolish mistakes from rushing.

b. I thought it would take me 30 minutes to get to my friend's house, but I _____ when I took a wrong turn and it took almost an hour.

c. When you take an international flight, you have to get to the airport at least two hours in advance. I usually _____ by reading or talking on my cell phone.

d. Cary Grant and Grace Kelly, movie stars from the 1950s and 60s, were famous _____ and I have never seen any of their movies.

e. My English language teachers often tell me that if I read a lot in English and watch a lot of English language movies, _____ I will understand much more.

f. Even though I know you shouldn't eat too many sweets, _____ I enjoy eating dessert after dinner. I think it is OK as long as you don't have dessert every day.

Warm Up

Look at the two cartoons then answer the questions.

a. Do you find cartoon 1 funny?   YES / NO
b. Do you find cartoon 2 funny?   YES / NO
c. Cartoon 1 makes fun of   MEN / WOMEN
d. Cartoon 2 makes fun of   MEN / WOMEN
e. Do you think this is what men and women really think about each other?

The man women want   The man who wants a women

Reading Strategy: Understanding purpose and tone

Most texts aim to inform (describe or analyze), persuade (influence or convince), and/or entertain (amuse). Knowing the text's **purpose**—or why the writer has written the text—will help you understand what you are reading.

Identifying the text's **tone**—or the writer's attitude and feelings towards the subject of the text—will also help you understand what you are reading. The tone might be formal, informal, humorous, angry, enthusiastic, critical, etc. When reading, consider the words the writer chooses, the way he or she writes, and any opinions in the text.

Purpose and **tone** are closely linked. If the purpose of a text is to inform, the tone will usually be formal, and objective. If the purpose is to persuade, the tone is more emotional, and it might even be angry or enthusiastic. Entertaining texts are usually informal and emotional. A text with a formal or serious tone will usually include long sentences, and have more complicated language, such as "provide" instead of "give," or "include" instead of "have."

Most texts may have more than one purpose and tone, so you should use your judgment to understand the writer's intention, attitude, and feelings.

Strategy in Focus

1 Read the text and decide its main purpose.

a. to inform   **b.** to persuade   **c.** to entertain

Student's Failed Bank Robbery

An art student tried to rob the Township Bank in Austin, Texas, to pay for his tuition fees. He walked into the bank and wrote a note saying, "Thiz iz a robbury. Put all yur muney in thiz bag." Not only was his plan bad, but he could not spell either! While standing in line for the bank teller, he began to worry that someone had seen him write the note, and that they might call the police. So, he left the Township Bank and crossed the street to the City Savings Bank.

After waiting in line at the City Savings Bank, he handed his note to the bank teller. The teller read it and thought, "How dumb is this guy?" She told him she could not accept his note because it was written on Township Bank paper and advised him to go back to the Township Bank.

Looking confused, the student said, "OK" and left! The City Savings Bank teller called the police immediately. The police arrested the man a few minutes later as he was waiting in line back at the Township Bank. At least the student will now have plenty of time to improve his spelling–in jail!

2 The tone of this article is:

a. serious   **b.** humorous   **c.** angry

3 Underline the parts of the text that indicate its tone.

Feedback:

The main purpose of the text is to entertain. It is taken from a website called 'Strange but True Stories.' The story is also about a student who does something stupid, and it ends with a joke.

Although the subject of this article—an attempted bank robbery—is serious, the tone is humorous. Clues that the text is informal are the use of shorter sentences, exclamation marks, and informal language, such as the cashier thinking, "How dumb is this guy?"

Before Reading

1 You are going to read a text about how people from the West often think differently to Asians. Skim the text and decide its tone.

    a. formal and serious   **b.** informal and angry   **c.** informal and humorous

2 Look at the picture. What can you see? Decide which description is closest to your first thought.

    a. There is a fish tank.   **b.** There are three big fish.   **c.** There is some seaweed and fish.

3 Read the beginning of the text below. What do you think is the purpose of the text?

The way the mind works is heavily influenced by culture, according to University of Michigan psychologist Richard Nisbett, author of *The Geography of Thought: How Asians and Westerners Think Differently ... and Why.*

    a. To persuade the reader it is better to think like a Westerner.
    b. To inform the reader how Asians and Westerners think differently.
    c. To entertain the reader with a story about an Asian and an American.

While Reading

4 Read the text and decide if you were correct about its purpose and tone.

After Reading

5 Look at your answer to activity 2. Tell a partner if you are more of a Western or an Asian thinker.

6 Check [✓] the inferences you can make about the text.

    a. _____ Americans do not understand East Asian people.
    b. _____ Americans and East Asians are taught to think in different ways by their family, friends, and school.
    c. _____ Americans cannot understand feelings and relationships.
    d. _____ Americans and East Asians described the fish and the fish tank differently because they are taught to think think in different ways by their cultures.
    e. _____ Americans and East Asians cannot work or study together.

Eastern and Western Thinking

The way the mind works is heavily influenced by culture, according to University of Michigan psychologist Richard Nisbett, author of *The Geography of Thought: How Asians and* [5] *Westerners Think Differently ... and Why.*

Richard Nisbett says that two people from different cultures can look at the same picture and see it in different ways. Culture also teaches people how to see and describe their experiences. [10] Nisbett explains that Asians think differently to Westerners because their culture teaches them to be more aware of society, family, and historical context. Western culture—and especially American culture—tends to pay more attention [15] to individual success and being independent of family.

Nisbett argues that culture makes East Asians more holistic or global thinkers: When trying to understand a situation, they like to see the whole [20] picture. They trust feelings and attach significance to relationships because these are valued highly in their culture.

Conversely, Nisbett's research has shown that Westerners tend to be more analytical. When they [25] try to understand something, Westerners usually prefer to analyze small pieces of information first and build their knowledge piece by piece in order to understand the whole picture.

In study after study, Nisbett and colleagues [30] from China, Korea, and Japan found that East Asians and Americans responded in different ways to the same situation. In one experiment, Japanese and Americans viewed the same animated underwater scenes, and reported [35] what they had seen.

In the experiment, most of the Americans started by explaining the details, for example, saying there were large fish in the front on the right. However, the Japanese talked about the [40] environment or context, first, mentioning that there is a pond or a fish tank. The Japanese also talked more about the environment and inanimate objects than the Americans, for example, "The big fish swam past the gray [45] seaweed."

This research confirms the traditional idea that Americans are less interested in social context and place importance on the individual. The Japanese, on the other hand, place more [50] importance on social context.

Word Work

7 Complete the sentences with a word chunk from the text. Change the tense if necessary.

heavily influenced by	tend to be	pay attention to (something)
piece by piece	be less interested in (something)	

  a. Nisbett believes that Americans _____ analytic and East Asians are holistic.

  b. According to the article, Americans _____ relationships and feelings.

  c. Do you agree that East Asians _____ the feelings of others more than Americans?

  d. Do you agree that East Asians are _____ their social context and relationships?

  e. If you are an analytic thinker, you analyze something _____ .

Before Reading

1 Read the title of the text. What is the purpose of the text?

a. To inform the reader of the advantages and disadvantages of single sex schools.
b. To entertain the reader with a funny story about the writer's school.
c. To persuade the reader that boys and girls should not study together.

2 Check [✓] the advantages of single sex schools you think will be mentioned in the text.

a. _____ Students can concentrate better.
b. _____ Girls have more opportunities to talk in class.
c. _____ There is less peer pressure.
d. _____ There are fewer discipline problems.
e. _____ Boys are less distracted.
f. _____ Students are less shy/more confident.
g. Add your own ideas:

While Reading

3 Which advantages of single sex schools can you find in the text? As you read, confirm your answers in activity 2.

4 Decide what tone the author uses. Check [✓] your answers.

a. _____ formal
b. _____ humorous
c. _____ informal
d. _____ enthusiastic
e. _____ critical
f. _____ serious

After Reading

5 Underline any statements in the text you agree with and double underline any statements you disagree with. Tell a partner which of the author's arguments about single sex schools you do and do not agree with.

6 Decide if the statements are true (T) or false (F), according to the text.

a. T F The author thinks single sex schools are better than coed schools.
b. T F The part of the brain that helps us understand our emotions grows slower in boys.
c. T F Jack White doesn't like his all-boys school.
d. T F Adolescent boys' and girls' brains develop at the same rate.
e. T F Women teachers usually need to talk louder to boys.
f. T F Jack doesn't like to study poetry in his new school.

CD 1:
Track 12

Separate Boys and Girls at School

Jack White is a 17-year-old student who has already published a collection of poetry with a local publisher. Jack believes switching to an all-boys' school from his coed high school [5] changed his life.

"When I was at my coed school, poetry was for girls not boys. Guys were supposed to like subjects like math, computers, and science. When I wrote poems, the guys at school used [10] to make fun of me and girls did not want to date me. At my new school, things are different. Boys are not wasting their time acting tough to impress the girls, and I don't worry what girls are thinking since there aren't any."

[15] Jack may not realize that boys and girls also learn and think differently based on specific biological developments. These differences affect how and when boys and girls learn, so single-sex education is actually better for [20] children.

Take, for example, brain development. The areas of the brain involved in language, feelings, physical coordination, and social relationships, develop in a different order and speed in girls [25] and boys. Adolescent girls find it easier to answer the question, "How does the story make you feel?" than adolescent boys. Research has shown that adolescent girls' brains develop the connections between language and emotions [30] earlier than boys' brains. An adolescent boy will have more difficulty answering that question because his brain has not fully developed that connection yet. In a single-sex classroom, everyone's brain is developing at similar speeds, [35] so teachers can teach according to their students' actual abilities.

Boys and girls also have different hearing abilities. Girls have a sense of hearing which is two to four times better than boys. Female [40] teachers often speak more quietly, so boys may have more difficulty hearing a female teacher if she is talking in her "normal" voice. The teacher needs to speak louder to get the boys' attention. In a single sex school, teachers do [45] not have to keep adjusting the volume of their voice.

Jack might not be aware of the biological arguments why single-sex education is better, but he realizes that he is learning faster at his [50] new school. As Jack says, "I hated writing and studying English in my old coed school, but look at me now, I am a published poet! My new school helped me become comfortable with who I really am."

Word Work

7 **Correct the mistakes in these word chunks.**

a. My elder brother used to **make funny of me** for believing in Santa Claus until I was 12.

b. He thought I **wasted my hours** writing letters to Santa Claus telling him what I wanted for Christmas.

c. However, as a young child, I thought it was the perfect way to **take** Santa's **attention**.

d. I **didn't trouble** what my brother said because my parents said Santa would bring me presents.

e. When I realized that my brother was right and Santa Claus wasn't real, **it touched my life**.

Before Reading

1 Skim the text and decide its tone. Check [✓] your answers.

a. _____ serious   b. _____ critical   c. _____ humorous   d. _____ optimistic

e. _____ formal   f. _____ sad   g. _____ informal   h. _____ angry

2 What is the purpose of the text?

a. A newspaper article to inform women how to meet the perfect man.

b. A textbook article to persuade the reader that men are more perfect than women.

c. A story to entertain the reader about a woman who is looking for the perfect man.

While Reading

3 Decide if you are correct about the text's purpose and tone.

After Reading

4 What do you think of the text? Check [✓] your answers. The text is:

a. _____ funny.   b. _____ realistic.   c. _____ boring.   d. _____ stupid.   e. _____ surprising.

5 Underline the parts of the text that indicate its tone.

6 Decide if you agree [✓] or disagree [×] with the interpretations of these sentences.

	Interpretation	✓ / ×
a. "they decided to catch up" (line 7)	They decided to find out what happened in each other's lives.	
b. "Finally, the topic turned to marriage." (line 11)	Mary and Sara started to talk about marriage.	
c. "I've been waiting for the perfect man." (line 24)	Sara was waiting in the coffee shop for her boyfriend.	
d. "I was beginning to give up on marriage." (line 43)	Sara was getting a divorce.	
e. "Apparently, he was looking for the perfect woman!" (line 52)	The man didn't want to marry Sara.	

**CD 1:
Track 13**

The Perfect Man!

Mary and Sara had been friends since childhood, but they had lost touch with each other when they went to different colleges. After living in different countries for most of their lives, they [5] both ended up living in the same city. One day, they bumped into each other on the bus and they decided to catch up over a coffee.

They spent most of the evening talking and laughing about their childhood memories, their [10] adventures living abroad, and their careers. Finally, the topic turned to marriage.

"So, whatever happened to you and Josh? Did the two of you tie the knot?" Sara asked.

Mary said that yes, they had been married for [15] 20 years and had two beautiful girls, Anna and Cecelia, who were now in high school. She could not be happier with her life.

"What about you? I remember you were popular with the boys in high school. There were a lot of [20] guys interested in you!" Mary said.

"Yeah, life has been interesting, but I'm not married." Sara replied.

"Why not?" asked Mary.

"Well, I've been waiting for the perfect man. [25] Right after I graduated from college, I met this great guy. I thought he was the one, but when I was transferred to India for work, he didn't want to leave his family and friends so we parted."

"That's too bad—you must have felt dreadful. [30] But I suppose he wasn't the perfect man after all," said Mary.

"It wasn't so bad because I was young and I was too busy with work to really commit myself to a serious relationship. My company then transferred [35] me to Italy and when I was there I met this really smart Italian guy. We dated for a few years, but eventually I realized he was too serious for me. I couldn't marry someone who didn't have a good sense of humor."

[40] "That's a shame, but he wasn't the perfect man either," Mary sighed.

"Yes, and by this time I was in my late thirties and I was beginning to give up on marriage. I was living in England and I was working really [45] hard. In fact, I was spending almost all my time at my office. I thought I was destined to live my life alone, but then one night, I met the perfect man. He was intelligent, sophisticated, successful, and loved to have fun. He was everything I had [50] been looking for."

"So, what happened?"

"Apparently, he was looking for the perfect woman!"

Word Work

7 **Match the word chunk with its definition.**

a. lose touch with someone •
b. bump into each other •
c. tie the knot •
d. be the one •

• i. be the perfect person to marry
• ii. meet someone by accident
• iii. not speak or see someone for a long time
• iv. get married

Reflection

▶ Which was your favorite text in this unit? Why?

▶ Which reading strategies did you use in this unit?

▶ Which new word chunks will you make an effort to use in the next five days? Choose at least five.

Our Emotions

Warm Up

1 Match each face with one of the emotions.

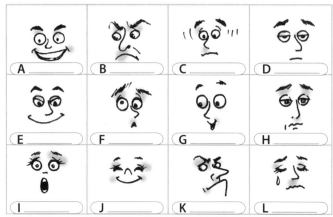

a. angry	b. bored	c. confused
d. confident	e. aggressive	f. depressed
g. curious	h. frightened/scared	i. happy
j. jealous	k. sad	l. worried

2 Decide which emotions are positive (+) and which are negative (-).

3 Tell a partner which emotions you have felt today.

Reading Strategy: Separating fact from opinion

Writers often mix fact and opinion together in an argument, so it is important that the reader is able to understand the difference between them.

Facts are statements that everyone can agree are true, and can be proven. In a text, examples of facts are names, places, numbers, dates, and times.

Opinions, on the other hand, are judgments, and a reader may not have the same opinion as the writer. To find a writer's opinion, you can look for words such as:

• Value adjectives, such as "great," "kind," "evil," etc.
• Adverbs, such as "moreover," "yet," "so," "certainly," etc.
• Verbs, such as "believe," "think," "consider," etc.

For example, the statement, "February is the shortest month of the year." is a fact. Whereas, "February in London is depressing as it is so cold and gray." is an opinion. You can argue opinions, but not facts.

Strategy in Focus

1 Decide if the statements are facts (F) or opinion (O).

   a. _____ Speaking English is difficult.
   b. _____ English is spoken in America and Canada, but the spelling of some words is different. For example, in America they write "color" and in Canada it is "colour."
   c. _____ There are around 400 million native speakers of English and about 500 million people who speak English as a second language.
   d. _____ The best way to learn English is by spending a year in an English-speaking country.
   e. _____ English is the official or co-official language of more than 45 countries, from Antigua to Zimbabwe.

Feedback:

   a. This is an opinion because some people would disagree. They might think speaking English is easy. It is possible to have a different opinion.
   b. This is a fact because we can demonstrate it is true. We can look in an American dictionary and a Canadian dictionary and see the same word is spelled differently.
   c. This is a fact because English language experts agree with these numbers. The number of English speakers in the world can be calculated.
   d. This is an opinion because some people would disagree. They might say the best way to learn English is to study hard. We cannot prove this is the best way to learn English.
   e. This is a fact because we can check the number of countries that use English as an official language in an encyclopedia or on reputable Internet sites.

2 Decide if the bold statements in this news story are fact (F) or opinion (O).

   a. _____ **b.** _____ **c.** _____ **d.** _____ **e.** _____

Denmark is the Happiest Place in the World.

(a) **Moving to Denmark will make you a happy person** according to an English scientist, Adrian White. (b) **Eighty thousand people, from all over the world, responded to his survey.** White reports that (c) **Switzerland and Austria came second and third in the survey, and Zimbabwe and Burundi came bottom.** White believes that (d) **a nation's happiness depends on its level of health.** He also says that (e) **wealth and education are important to many people's happiness.** White does not believe that the stress of modern life has as much influence on our happiness as people think.

Feedback:
The correct answers are: a. O; b. F; c. F; d. O; e. O

Before Reading

1 Answer these questions to decide your level of emotional intelligence.

   a. YES / NO   Do you feel uncomfortable telling people that you are feeling shy, sad, or angry?
   b. YES / NO   Do you find it difficult to start projects or work?
   c. YES / NO   When you feel depressed or bad, do you know the reasons?
   d. YES / NO   Are you usually bored at school or work?
   e. YES / NO   Are you only happy with your work when someone else likes it?

If you answered "no" to most of the questions, you probably have a high emotional intelligence.

2 Scan the text on the opposite page to find the best definition of emotional intelligence below.

   a. People with high emotional intelligence get straight As in their school exams.
   b. People with high emotional intelligence make a lot of money for commercial businesses.
   c. People with high emotional intelligence know how they and other people are feeling.

While Reading

3 As you read the text, decide if you need to improve your own emotional intelligence.

After Reading

4 What is your opinion of emotional intelligence? Tell a partner:
   a. if you think emotional intelligence is important.
   b. if you want to improve your emotional intelligence.

5 Decide if the bold statements (a-g) in the text are fact (F) or opinion (O) according to the writer.

   a. _____   **b.** _____   **c.** _____   **d.** _____
   e. _____   **f.** _____   **g.** _____

6 Decide if the bold statements (i-iv) in the text are fact (F) or opinion (O) according to Jesse.

   i. _____   **ii.** _____   **iii.** _____   **iv.** _____

CD 1:
Track 14

Emotional Intelligence

(a) **Jesse Brooks was a straight-A student—** a result of countless hours spent studying during college. She graduated at the top of her class and (i) **believed she would have no problem**

[5] **getting a job.** However, after ten interviews and no job offers, she was starting to wonder what was wrong. "At first I couldn't understand it, I mean, (ii) **I'm intelligent and diligent,** why couldn't I get a job?" Despite having "academic"

[10] intelligence, Jesse was missing the intelligence that many employers are now looking for, emotional intelligence.

(b) **Emotional intelligence (EI) is the ability to understand your own emotions and the**

[15] **emotions of people around you.** (c) **More and more companies use EI assessment tests to recruit new staff.** They have found that people with high EI form better relationships with their colleagues and can manage

[20] themselves better. (d) **This benefits the company**, in the form of higher productivity and profit.

For example, the French cosmetics company, (e) **L'Oreal, started to track the emotional**

[25] **intelligence of its employees in relation to their productivity.** Their studies showed that (f) **employees with high EI scores sold goods worth in total almost $100,000 more than their colleagues with low EI scores.** Clearly,

[30] employees with high emotional intelligence are more valuable to their companies.

Jesse thinks that she spent so much of her college life studying alone that (iii) **her social skills did not develop well.** Determined to get

[35] straight As, (iv) **she had not played any team sports or participated in any school groups**, both of which would have helped develop social skills and emotional intelligence. Although she could motivate herself to accomplish a goal, she

[40] did not know how to work with others, a key to success in most commercial businesses.

Although Jesse might not have a high EI now, psychologists believe (g) **she can improve it.** Jesse says, "I need to identify people who are

[45] "natural" leaders, who work well with others and are great motivators. I should watch what they say and how they act in different situations. Then go out, socialize, and try it out in my own life."

Word Work

7 Rewrite the sentences using the word chunks below.

| social skills | get a job | motivate herself | work well with others | try it out |

a. As a student, Jesse Brooks got good grades, but as an adult she couldn't **find work**.

b. She was very independent and could **force herself** to get her work done on time.

c. However, Jesse needed help learning how to **collaborate with people**.

d. She decided to learn how to work better with others and **practice it** in her own life.

e. Jesse developed better **interpersonal abilities** and became more successful at her job.

An Unbelievable Journey

Before Reading

1 Look at the title and the picture then skim the text. What is the story about?

a. A great holiday.
b. A story some people think is not true.
c. Some fishermen catching very big fish.

While Reading

2 As you read each paragraph, decide if the bold statements (a.- f.) are fact (F) or opinion (O).

a. _____   b. _____   c. _____   d. _____   e. _____   f. _____

After Reading

3 Tell a partner if you believe the fishermen's story.

4 According to their story, how did the survivors feel during their journey?

a. happy	b. bored	c. desperate	d. hopeful	e. frightened
f. curious	g. relieved	h. jealous	i. excited	j. depressed

5 What did you think about while you were reading the text? Write "Yes" if you made the association or "No" if you didn't.

Paragraph	Associations	Yes / No
2	a. A boat trip I have taken.	
	b. A time I had problems on a trip.	
	c. Why I don't like to travel by boat.	
5	a. A time I was helped by strangers.	
	b. A time I helped strangers.	
	c. A time I was really hungry and needed to eat.	
6	a. A time I was lost or someone I know was lost.	
	b. Bad weather conditions I have experienced.	
	c. A time I lost weight.	

6 Check [✓] the inferences you can make about the text.

a. _____ The survivors have different stories about how they became lost.
b. _____ Two fishermen died of food poisoning.
c. _____ Some people don't believe they were lost because they looked so healthy.
d. _____ Some people believe the three surviving fishermen ate their two friends.

An Unbelievable Journey

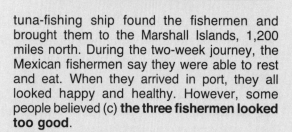

[1] Three fishermen lost at sea for 289 days (a) **landed 5,500 miles from where they started**, but is their story really true?

[2] On October 28, 2005 (b) **five fishermen left the coast of Mexico** on a three-day fishing trip. It was a sunny day, but things changed as night fell. A storm came in making it difficult to find the fishing nets they had left in the water. The boat soon ran out of fuel and the men became frightened as they drifted out to sea, unable to get back to the shore.

[3] Their small boat had no shelter, no navigational equipment, and held only a small amount of food and water. Desperate to stay alive, the men drank turtle blood and rainwater, and ate raw fish and birds. The survivors say that two of the men had trouble eating, eventually dying of starvation. They threw the bodies overboard.

[4] They tried not to lose hope, but life on a small boat can be boring, scary, and depressing. To keep their spirits up and their minds off the sharks that occasionally bumped against the boat, they sang traditional songs, read the Bible, and kept hoping for a miracle.

[5] One of the fishermen said, "We saw many boats pass by us. When that happened, it was depressing and we didn't talk for hours. But I never imagined we would die." It took over nine months but his optimism paid off. A Taiwanese tuna-fishing ship found the fishermen and brought them to the Marshall Islands, 1,200 miles north. During the two-week journey, the Mexican fishermen say they were able to rest and eat. When they arrived in port, they all looked happy and healthy. However, some people believed (c) **the three fishermen looked too good**.

[6] In all the historical records of sailors lost at sea, (d) **the longest someone had been missing was 76 days**. When that man was rescued, he was extremely thin and it took him months to recover. However, the three rescued fishermen, missing for much longer, did not have any of the noticeable health problems that would have been expected.

[7] Some experts argue (e) **it is almost impossible for their boat to have floated from Mexico** in a northern direction to the Marshall Islands as quickly as it did. Many think (f) **the fishermen were actually involved in an illegal smuggling operation** that went wrong. Others wonder what really happened to the two fishermen who did not survive. The fishermen insist they are telling the truth, but many question their story.

Word Work

7 Make word chunks from the story, using the verbs in the box.

run	have	lose	throw	tell

a. _____ (something) overboard   b. _____ out of gas

c. _____ hope   d. _____ trouble

e. _____ the truth

Before Reading

1 You are going to read a story about a teenage boy who works in his family's restaurant. How do you think the boy feels about:

a. the restaurant business.	love / hate / no feeling
b. his university graduation.	nervous / calm / impatient
c. getting a cookbook as a graduation present.	angry / happy / disappointed

2 Read the beginning of the story below. Predict how the sentence will end.

"Can I take your order?" Night after night, I had to repeat this phrase as I waited tables in my family's restaurant. My father was a famous chef and the restaurant was always packed, so I was always busy. My father loved cooking and spent most of his time in the kitchen. He wanted me to cook with him, but I …

a. was too lazy.   **b.** hated the restaurant business.   **c.** was scared of my father.

While Reading

3 Read the story and check your hypotheses and prediction.

After Reading

4 Tell a partner how the story made you feel.

5 Decide if the bold statements in the text are fact (F) or the writer's opinion (O).
a. _____   b. _____   c. _____   d. _____   e. _____

6 Choose the correct ending for each statement.
a. The writer didn't like his family's business because:
   i.   he didn't like to work hard.
   ii. he couldn't spend time with his friends and with his father.
b. The writer was happy before graduation because:
   i.   he was spending time with his father.
   ii. his father bought him a new car.
c. The writer was angry with his father on graduation day because:
   i.   he had to cook in the restaurant and he didn't like to cook.
   ii. he got a cookbook for a present and not a car.
d. The writer was sad at the end of the story because:
   i.   he found out his graduation present was a check to buy a car.
   ii. he had to go back home and work in the family business.

The Family Cookbook

"Can I take your order?" Night after night, I had to repeat this phrase as I waited tables in my family's restaurant. My father was a famous chef and the restaurant was always packed, so I was [5] always busy. My father loved cooking and spent most of his time in the kitchen. He wanted me to cook with him, but I hated the restaurant business. Because of the restaurant, I never had a social life, and while other fathers would play [10] soccer with their sons, my father was always busy. I thought (a) **he was more concerned about his food than what I was doing**.

Throughout high school and college, I worked with my family, but always avoided the kitchen [15] area and my father. I was impatient to graduate so I could move away from the family business and start my own life. As graduation day drew near, my father and I started looking at new cars. It was the first time that I remembered my father [20] spending time with me outside the restaurant. The week before graduation we found the perfect car. I was sure that (b) **my father would buy it** and give it to me on graduation night.

On the night of graduation, (c) **my father handed** [25] **me a gift-wrapped book**. It was my father's old, food-stained cookbook. I was so angry that I threw the cookbook down and stormed out of the house. I could not believe that with all of his money and all of the time that I had spent working [30] in the restaurant, all I would get was that old cookbook. Plus, he knew I hated cooking!

I soon moved away and after many years became successful in my own business. Although I often saw my father at holidays, our relationship was [35] strained and (d) **we never talked about the graduation gift**. Then one day, I got a call that my father was in hospital. I went to see him because I was very anxious and wanted to make sure he would be OK.

[40] That night at my parents' home, I was looking through my father's books with my mother. I came across the cookbook that he had given me years ago. I carefully opened the cookbook, filled with my father's handwritten notes, and went through the [45] pages. Midway through, I found something that made my eyes fill with tears. It was a check, dated the day of my graduation, (e) **made out in the exact amount needed for the car** we had picked out all those years ago.

Word Work

7 Circle the correct word chunk.

a. I **waited people / waited tables** in my family's restaurant.
b. I wanted to **move away from / leave away from** home and start my own business.
c. My father always **spent most of his time / gave most of his time** in the kitchen.
d. As I was going through the food-stained cookbook, I **came onto/came across** a check.

Reflection

▶ Which was your favorite text in this unit? Why?

▶ Which reading strategies did you use in this unit?

▶ Which new word chunks will you make an effort to use in the next five days? Choose at least five.

6 Misunderstandings

Warm Up

Look at the pictures. Tell a partner about each cultural misunderstanding.

a. In America, people shake hands, but in Korea...   **b.** In America, young men sometimes hug each other, but in Japan...

c. In America, it is acceptable to..., but in Japan...   **d.** In Thailand, it is rude to...

Reading Strategy: Understanding references

Most texts are full of **references**. Reference words such as "she," "his," "her," "himself," "those," "which," and "both" usually refer to nouns that have appeared earlier in the text. They can sometimes refer to nouns appearing later in a text.

For example, "Italy won the World Cup in 2006. It was the second time they had won it. Both teams in the final, Italy and France, had won the World Cup before."

* "They" and "it" replace the nouns Italy and World Cup. The writer doesn't need to repeat Italy and World Cup and uses the references "they" and "it" instead.

* The phrase, "Both teams," refers to Italy and France. The words "Italy" and "France" appear later in the text.

It is important to understand what word(s) a **reference** substitutes to understand a text. Identifying the correct word(s) for a reference is also a useful test-taking skill because tests such as TOEFL and TOEIC ask questions to test this knowledge.

To find the word (or words) a **reference** refers to, read the sentence where the reference appears, and then read the previous sentence or two again. To confirm you have identified the correct word for the reference, substitute the word for the reference. If the substitution is logical, you have probably identified the correct word.

Strategy in Focus

1 **Read the letter. How many reference words does it contain?**

a. none **b.** 12 **c.** 18 **d.** 24 **e.** 30 **f.** 36

Dear Agatha,

Growing up, my closest friends were Sam and Jill. **We** did everything together and were even roommates in college. After graduation we all moved to different cities and our friendship changed, **which** I thought was normal as we were busy with our jobs, working a lot of overtime. To be honest, I saw Sam more often because **she** sometimes worked in my city.

However, just the other day, Sam phoned and asked if I was planning to go to Jill's wedding. I had no idea she was getting married and I certainly didn't get an invitation. I thought this was strange since I invited them **both** to my wedding a few years ago and we seemed to have a great time. **Everyone**—my family and my husband's family—made her feel welcome.

Sam thinks that Jill must have invited me but the invitation got lost in the mail. I don't know what to do. Maybe she just doesn't want to invite me since **we** haven't been in touch for a few years. I'm very upset. What should I do?

Thanks,
Teresa

2 **Find these words in the text. What do they refer to?**

a. we (line 2):
  i. Agatha and Teresa   **ii.** Sam and Jill   **iii.** Teresa, Sam, and Jill

b. which (line 5):
  i. college graduation   **ii.** friendship changed   **iii.** moving another city

c. she (line 7):
  i. Sam   **ii.** Jill   **iii.** Teresa

d. both (line 13):
  i. Sam and Jill   **ii.** Jill and Teresa   **iii.** Agatha and Teresa

e. everyone (line 14):
  i. Teresa and Tim   **ii.** Jill's family   **iii.** Teresa and Tim's families

f. we (line 18):
  i. Sam and Jill   **ii.** Jill and Teresa   **iii.** Teresa, Sam and Jill

Feedback:

1. answer = e. The referencing words you should have noted are: my, We, we, our, I, we, our, I, she, my, I, I, she, I, I, this, I, them both, my, we, my, my, her, me, I, she, me, we, I'm, I.
2. answers = a. iii; b. ii; c. i; d. i; e. iii; f. ii.

Before Reading

1 Look at the title and the picture then read the first paragraph. What is the story about?
   a. Students do not use correct spelling in their emails.
   b. Professors do not know how to use email correctly.
   c. Students can be too informal in their emails.

2 Skim the text and check your hypothesis. Underline statements that confirm your hypothesis.

While Reading

3 As you read the text, decide if you agree [✓] or disagree [×] with the interpretations of the underlined words.

Text	Interpretation	✓ / ×
a. "Ask Professor Harding what he thinks of emails and <u>you get an earful</u>." (line 1)	The professor is unhappy about student emails and has a lot to say about it.	
b. "Franklin had to explain to her students that emails had to be written in formal, standard English, and <u>be professional or business-like in tone</u>." (line 21)	Franklin thinks students should write emails to businesses to get a job.	
c. "<u>Emailing my question is much more comfortable for me</u>, plus I feel like I don't inconvenience him." (line 38)	I can email from home in a comfortable chair or wearing pajamas.	
d. "He can get back to me <u>when it's good for him</u>." (line 40)	at a convenient time for the professor	

After Reading

4 Tell a partner if you prefer to email or talk to your teacher and if you will change the way you email teachers.

5 Complete these sentences using a reference word from the box.

that	who	him	he	another

Ask Professor Harding what _____ thinks of emails and you get an earful. He will tell you about the incident of the student _____ skipped class and then sent him an email asking for the class notes. In another incident, a student got angry at him for not responding to an urgent email because he did not realize that the professor's Internet access was down. Another emailed _____ at 2 a.m. to ask for the research paper topic _____ was due at 10 a.m.

The Trouble with Email

Ask Professor Harding what he thinks of emails and you get an earful. He will tell you about the incident of the student who skipped class and then sent him an email asking for the class
[5] notes. In another incident, a student got angry at him for not responding to an urgent email because she did not realize that the professor's Internet access was down.

Email has become an accepted and expected
[10] way to keep in touch with professors at universities, and when done correctly, can help students and professors communicate. However, some professors are finding that it can also cause major misunderstandings.

[15] Informality and inappropriateness are the causes of many misunderstandings in emails. Another professor, Professor Franklin, had one student who thought it was acceptable to use slang and a very informal, familiar tone in his messages.
[20] The email started with, "Wazzup, Teach?" and ended with "Peace." Franklin had to explain to her students that emails had to be written in formal, standard English, and be professional or business-like in tone.

[25] Additional problems occur when the tone of a message is misunderstood. One student emailed a professor asking why he got a B on his paper. The professor thought the student was unhappy with the grade, but in fact the student was
[30] pleased—he wanted to know what he had done well, so he could do it again for the next paper. Unlike oral communication, email cannot convey tone of voice and facial expressions.

Email, however, is mostly a positive tool for
[35] students and their professors. Andrea, a college student agreed, "I'm pretty shy, so if I had to go to my professor's office whenever I didn't understand something, I wouldn't go. Emailing my question is much more comfortable for me,
[40] plus I feel like I don't inconvenience him. He can get back to me when it's good for him."

These days, most professors give out their email addresses so students can stay in touch, and—like Professor Franklin—they set up
[45] guidelines at the beginning of the semester. As for Professor Harding, he no longer puts his email address on the class syllabus; only his office phone number is listed.

Word Work

6 **Correct the mistakes in these word chunks.**

a. Jason hadn't done his homework, so he decided to **skip lesson** and went to the beach instead.

_____

b. I couldn't use my email this weekend because my **Internet access was out of order**.

_____

c. Email has almost replaced the phone call as the **accepted and predictable way** for keeping in touch with people.

_____

d. I use email to **keep in communication** with my friends more than I use my cell phone.

_____

e. The Internet lets me **stay in feeling** with my friends and family who live overseas.

_____

Before Reading

1 Decide if you agree [✓] or disagree [×] with these statements.

a. _____ It is easier to talk to men than women.

b. _____ Men talk more than women.

c. _____ I argue more with men than women.

d. _____ Women talk more about their feelings than men.

2 Take two minutes to skim the text. What is it about?

a. The way men and women drive is different.

b. The way men and women talk is different.

c. Men and women get angry for different reasons.

While Reading

3 As you read the text, check your answer to question 2. Underline any statements that confirm it.

After Reading

4 Associate the text with your personal experiences. Answer these questions.

a. The last time you saw your best friend, what did you talk about?

b. What do you talk about with your male friends? With your female friends?

c. Do you agree with Deborah Tannen? Think about people you know before you answer.

5 Find these words in the text. What do they refer to?

a. this (line 12): _____

b. she (line 23): _____

c. where (line 31): _____

d. who (line 36): _____

e. this (line 46): _____

f. their (line 50): _____

g. we (line 55): _____

h. our (line 56): _____

CD 1:
Track 18

How Men and Women Communicate

Emma and Ryan, a married couple, were driving to a friend's house when Emma turned to Ryan and asked, "Would you like to stop for lunch?"

[5] Ryan replied, "No, I'm not hungry yet." and continued driving. Meanwhile, Emma sat quietly fuming in the passenger seat. Ryan could not understand why Emma was irritated. He had thought she was asking if he was hungry, but [10] in reality, Emma was telling him that she was hungry and wanted to stop for lunch.

Misunderstandings like this often occur between the sexes, even among people from the same culture. Deborah Tannen, professor of [15] linguistics at Georgetown University in the United States, has studied conversational differences between men and women, and believes that some problems occur because men and women may grow up with different [20] conversational rules.

In Emma and Ryan's situation, Emma was making a request in the form of a question. Her style of talking is common for women. She needed Ryan to agree they were both hungry. So, Emma asked [25] Ryan what he wanted. She was really telling Ryan what she wanted, however, Ryan did not understand this. If he had been hungry, he would have said something more direct, such as, "I'm hungry, let's have lunch."

[30] Tannen believes that most women grow up in a world where talk is used to express feelings, to stay emotionally close to friends and partners, and to reach agreement. However, she believes that most men are raised differently and they tend [35] to keep their feelings to themselves.

Take the case of Alana and Oliver who have been dating for two years. Every day they meet for lunch and Alana sees this as an opportunity to talk and become close. However, she usually gets [40] frustrated because Oliver does not start much of the conversation, and instead is happy to eat in silence.

Tannen says, for men like Oliver, talk is often used as a contest, to be used outside the home [45] to gain respect, to entertain and get attention, and exchange information. This is why men communicate by making each other laugh, or talking about sport, and work. These men do not always feel it is necessary to talk to feel close or [50] to express their feelings. Women on the other hand, are encouraged to speak about their feelings since this is a way to build relationships.

It is no wonder that misunderstandings occur between men and women and as a result, [55] relationships become strained. Even though we might be speaking the same language, our conversational differences sometimes make it difficult to communicate effectively.

Word Work

6 Circle the correct word chunk.

a. My grandmother **grew up / raised up** in a world without computers.

b. Let's **join for lunch / meet for lunch** at 1:00 p.m.

c. After 40 years of marriage, my parents often **eat in silence / eat in quiet**.

d. My brother has **become familiar / become close** with many of his teammates on his hockey team.

e. My father doesn't talk about his emotions, instead he **holds his feelings to himself / keeps his feelings to himself**.

An Unwitting Bank Robber

Before Reading

1 Read the title and the first paragraph. What is the story about?

a. _____ A young woman called Freda, who runs slowly.

b. _____ Two bank robbers, Freda, and her mother.

c. _____ A young woman called Freda, who robs a bank by accident.

While Reading

2 As you read the text, visualize images in your mind.

After Reading

3 Circle the images you visualized in your mind. Describe them and any others you saw to a partner.

a mother and daughter talking	an envelope with money
a bank	some police officers

4 Check [✓] the inferences you can make about the story.

a. _____ Freda Lewis is forgetful.

b. _____ Freda was a bank robber.

c. _____ Freda drove a car to the bank.

d. _____ The teller thought Freda was a bank robber because she was wearing a ski mask.

e. _____ Freda asked the bank teller for $10,000.

5 Find these words in the text. What do they refer to?

a. one of her neighbors (line 2): _____

b. she (line 4): _____

c. who (line 24): _____

d. their (line 26): _____

e. the poor girl (line 28): _____

f. her (line 30): _____

g. someone (line 36): _____

h. everything (line 45): _____

An Unwitting Bank Robber

A friend once told me about an incident concerning one of her neighbors, Freda Lewis. Freda was known throughout town as a really popular young woman, but she sometimes behaved strangely [5] and she had a terrible memory. She was always forgetting something.

One day her mother asked Freda to go downtown to the bank because she needed some money. It was a really cold, windy, winter day, so Freda [10] dressed warmly. To be extra warm she put a ski mask on to protect her face from the cold wind. When she got to the bank, Freda forgot that she was still wearing the ski mask over her face and went inside.

[15] Freda walked up to the window, and the teller panicked because she saw a person wearing a ski mask. Without saying a word, the teller gave Freda $10,000 in an envelope. Freda did not check the envelope before leaving the bank and [20] had no clue she was carrying such a large fortune when she drove off.

Meanwhile, the teller called the police and said that her bank had just been held up by a robber who was wearing a ski mask. Freda was on her [25] way back home when she noticed that there were three police cars with their lights and sirens on behind her. The police forced her to stop and came out of their cars holding guns. The poor girl was confused and frightened to death, and [30] had no idea why the police would be after her. She held up her hands to surrender and the police pulled her out of the car and forced her to the ground.

When a police officer pulled off the ski mask, [35] they all recognized Freda, and realized that someone had made a mistake. Once the police explained why they were there, Freda told them that she always wore a ski mask when it was cold and that she must have forgotten she was [40] wearing it when she entered the bank.

When the police questioned the bank teller to ask if Freda had demanded the money, the teller realized that she had made a big mistake and had just assumed that Freda was a robber. [45] Luckily, no one was hurt, and everything was returned to the bank.

From that day forward, Freda no longer wears a ski mask when she is in a bank.

Word Work

6 Make word chunks from the story using the verbs in the box. Some verbs can be used more than once.

tell	walk	have	be	make

a. _____ no idea
b. _____ up to the window
c. _____ a mistake
d. _____ (someone) a story
e. _____ no clue
f. _____ confused

Reflection

▶ Which was your favorite text in this unit? Why?

▶ Which reading strategies did you use in this unit?

▶ Which new word chunks will you make an effort to use in the next five days? Choose at least five.

Review Reading Strategies

- Unit 4: Understanding purpose and tone
- Unit 5: Separating fact from opinion
- Unit 6: Understanding references

1 Read each statement and check [✓] the word that is being described.

	Purpose	Tone	Fact	Opinion	Reference
a. A word that replaces a noun that appears earlier or later in the text.					
b. A statement expressing an attitude about something.					
c. For example, describing a text as funny, serious, critical, or informal.					
d. The reason an author has written a text, for example, to persuade, inform, or entertain.					
e. A statement expressing something that has happened and it can be proved.					

2 Read the title of the text. What is the purpose of the text?

a. To inform the reader of why models are beautiful.
b. To consider how ideas of beauty vary.
c. To persuade the reader that thin people are beautiful.

3 Read the text and decide if you were correct about its purpose.

4 Decide which tones the author uses. Check [✓] your answers.

a. _____ formal   **b.** _____ humorous   **c.** _____ informal
d. _____ enthusiastic   **e.** _____ critical   **f.** _____ serious

5 As you read each paragraph, decide if each of the bold statements is fact (F) or opinion (O).

a. _____   **b.** _____   **c.** _____   **d.** _____   **e.** _____   **f.** _____

6 In paragraph 1, the word "they" refers to:

a. people   **b.** others   **c.** parents   **d.** models

Reading

CD 1:
Track 20

Is That Really Beautiful?

[1] There is a popular saying, "Don't judge a book by its cover", but people often judge others based on what **they** look like. (a) **In fact, it only takes about seven seconds for people to form a first impression of someone else and that impression is often about what we see.** Appearance and looking good is important for most people, but unfortunately, what we think is beautiful is often unrealistic. Just take a look at American magazines or television. Everywhere you look there are beautiful people who are extremely thin and unhealthily tanned.

[2] It is impossible to ignore that being really thin and tanned are marks of beauty for women in the USA. This got me thinking about how our definition of beauty has changed over the years and what other cultures think is beautiful.

[3] (b) **Although women in Hollywood and the West are obsessed with being too thin**, there was a point in our past when being plump was a sign of wealth and being fat was beautiful. (c) **If you look at the paintings by Botticelli, an Italian Renaissance painter, the women are full figured and curvy** because that was considered beautiful. Now, a toned, thin, fat-free body shows that you have time and money to work out or more likely, you can afford plastic surgery!

[4] Similarly, in Europe pale skin used to be another indicator of how much money you had since it showed that you didn't have to work outside in the fields. Nowadays, a tanned body is evidence that you have time to sunbathe on vacation. Because not all Americans can afford a beach vacation, they buy tanning creams that will darken their skin or go to tanning booths to get an artificial tan. (d) **In 2006, over 30 million Americans spent over 5 billion dollars at tanning salons, despite the warnings that it increases the risk of skin cancer. (e) It seems many Americans are ready to sacrifice everything to achieve that beautiful tanned look**.

[5] When I asked some of my international friends what they thought was beautiful I got some very different answers. For example, pale skin and light-colored eyes are desirable in many Asian countries so whitening creams and light-colored contacts are popular beauty products. (f) **In some African countries, like Nigeria, women are sent to fattening houses before their wedding** so they will look plump, which is considered to be beautiful. This seems to be the other extreme to the method of starving yourself in the West. I just wish we could all agree that a beautiful person is someone who is happy with themselves; but I guess that is too much to ask for in our beauty-obsessed world.

Comprehension Check

1   The word "obsessed" in paragraph 3 is closest in meaning to:

     a. disinterested   **b.** addicted   **c.** excited   **d.** upset

2   In paragraph 4, the author implies that the American habit of tanning can be:

     a. unhealthy   **b.** time consuming   **c.** addictive   **d.** relaxing

3   In paragraph 5, the author mentions Nigeria as an example of:

     a. a country that has strange ideas about beauty.
     b. a country that has a contrasting definition of beauty compared to the USA.
     c. a country that has a similar definition of beauty as the USA.
     d. a country that has an unhealthy idea of beauty.

4   Which of the following is NOT a sign of beauty mentioned in the text?

     a. having light colored eyes   **b.** having a toned body
     c. having straight hair   **d.** being plump

5   Check [✓] the inferences you can make about the text. Underline the words, phrases, or sentences that support your inferences.

     a. _____ The author doesn't like the current American definition of beauty.
     b. _____ Using tanning salons may lead to death.
     c. _____ Nigerian men believe that overweight women are beautiful.
     d. _____ Hollywood promotes the idea that being tanned is unhealthy.

More Word Chunks

1   Complete the word chunks

look	ignore	beauty	thinking	years

     a. This article **got me** _____ about what I believe is beautiful.
     b. Over the _____, I have spent a lot of money on creams to keep me looking young.
     c. However, it is **impossible to** _____ the lines around my eyes and the fact that I am getting older.
     d. Now I have a different definition of beautiful. I think kindness is **a mark of** _____.
     e. Take a _____ around you. What do you believe is beautiful?

2   Use these word chunks to write sentences about yourself or someone you know.

     a. lose touch with (someone): _____
     b. get (someone's) attention: _____
     c. lose hope: _____
     d. make fun of (someone/something): _____
     e. come across (something): _____

3 Here are some other word chunks made from "get," "lose," and "come."

get:	lost	in the way	caught
lose:	control	your mind	your cool (to become angry)
come:	home	out (to become available)	clean (to be honest about something)

Complete the sentences using any of the word chunks on pages 62 and 63. Change the verb tense when necessary

a. My friend plagiarized her paper but she **got** _____ and failed the class.

b. When going through old photos, I **came** _____ a picture of my parents when they got married.

c. When walking in Tokyo, I took a wrong turn and **got** _____.

d. I **lost** _____ at someone when they scratched the paint on my new car.

e. When the iPhone **came** _____, people were excited about the new design.

f. After I went away to college, I **lost** _____ with some of my high school friends.

Warm Up

What do you think is the toughest challenge? Rank these challenges from 1 (the toughest) to 4 (the least tough).

- **a.** _____ running a marathon (26 miles / 42 Km)
- **b.** _____ not eating or drinking for 24 hours
- **c.** _____ being the president of a country
- **d.** _____ becoming a martial arts expert

Reading Strategy: Highlighting and annotating

Highlighting the significant parts of a text while reading helps you to:

- read more carefully and maintain interest.
- distinguish important from unimportant information.
- remember important information.
- retrieve information later without rereading the whole text.

It is important to only **highlight** useful information and NOT to highlight too much. Some things that might be useful to highlight are definitions, names, dates, events, lists, causes and effects, similarities and differences, main ideas, summaries, and conclusions.

Annotations are brief notes written by the side of a text or in the page margin.
Annotating the text helps you keep your reading active, and like highlighting, making annotations helps to distinguish and retrieve important information. Annotations comprise:

- Key words—if a text contains a lot of facts, you can indicate in the margin where these facts appear. For example, next to statistics and facts about the population of Tokyo, you could write "Tokyo facts." Or, you could show where the main idea is by writing "main idea" in the margin.
- Your questions and comments—it is also useful to write your personal responses in the margins. You might write a thought or opinion like "this cannot be true" or "this is the same as my country."

Tip: It is a good idea to **skim** the text (see page 8) before highlighting or annotating.

Strategy in Focus

1 Look at the highlighted (underlined) text and annotations for the first paragraph of the text. Highlight and make annotations for the rest of the text.

Great Grandmother Still Studying

At the age of 95, <u>Nola Ochs became one of the world's oldest college graduates.</u> Ochs received her bachelor's degree in general studies and history at Fort Hays State University in 2007.

> I don't think we have that degree in our universities.

> Is this an American University?

At her graduation ceremony, the crowd gave her a standing ovation, breaking a rule against applauding until the names of all 2,176 graduates were read, a list that also included her granddaughter, Alexandra Ochs.

Relatives from as far away as California came to see Nola graduate. They wore "Nola's #1 Fans" T-shirts and they cheered and waved American flags as she walked across the stage.

Nola seemed a little embarrassed by all the attention. "I was just another student," Ochs said in a news conference after the graduation ceremony.

However, none of the other graduates was entered in the Guinness Book of Records as the world's oldest college graduate. The former record holder was Mozelle Richardson, who earned a degree from the University of Oklahoma in 2004 at the age of 90.

Ochs has a family that includes three sons—a fourth died in 1995—13 grandchildren and 15 great grandchildren.

She started taking classes occasionally in 1972 at Dodge City Community College after the death of her husband of 39 years, Vernon. After moving to Fort Hays in 2006, she completed the final 30 hours required for her degree.

A guest speaker at the graduation ceremony advised the students to "Follow the footsteps of people like Nola" and never give up.

2 Show a partner what you highlighted and what annotations you made.

Feedback:

Some key ideas you could have highlighted are:

a standing ovation; included her granddaughter, Alexandra Ochs; embarrassed, Guinness Book of Records as the world's oldest college graduate; 1972 at Dodge City Community College after the death of her husband of 39 years, Vernon; never give up.

You could have made annotations like:

How old was her granddaughter?; They should have waited to applaud.; Did she study because her husband died?; It took her more than 30 years to get her degree.; If she can study, so can I.

Before Reading

1 Tell a partner anything you know about marathons or monks.

2 Take two minutes to skim the text. What is it about?
a. Fujinami is a monk who is trying to complete an ancient Buddhist ritual called Kaihogyo.
b. Kaihogyo takes seven years to complete and if successful, it will result in spiritual enlightenment.

While Reading

3 Read the article quickly and without stopping. While reading, decide if your answer to activity 2 is correct.

After Reading

4 Highlight the key ideas in each paragraph.

5 Match the annotation to the paragraph.

Annotation	Paragraph
a. This may be used to commit suicide!	1, 2, 3, 4, 5
b. How many have failed?	1, 2, 3, 4, 5
c. I couldn't survive one day without food and water.	1, 2, 3, 4, 5
d. That is two marathons a day!	1, 2, 3, 4, 5

6 Choose the best ending to the summary.
The article, *The Marathon Monks*, explains the process called Kaihogyo that some Buddhist monks go through in the hope of reaching enlightenment.
a. It describes how Genshin Fujinami runs 18 miles a day for 1,000 days and also has to pray 260 times a day. He is only allowed some food, a candle, a prayer book, a rope, and a knife for his 25,800-mile run.
b. It describes in detail why the ritual is so physically and mentally demanding. Some of the challenges the monks face include running 25,800 miles in 1,000 days, which is on average almost a marathon a day, as well as praying 260 times a day, and going without food or water for seven days.

The Marathon Monks

[1] It is midnight and Genshin Fujinami puts on his white robe and handmade straw sandals, and sets off on a 21-mile (30 km) run around Mt. Hiei in Japan. Fujinami is a marathon monk who is trying to complete an ancient Buddhist ritual called *Kaihogyo*. It takes seven years to complete and he believes that if he is successful, he will get spiritual enlightenment. However, according to tradition, if Fujinami fails, he will have to take his own life – though he may stop the *Kaihogyo* under certain conditions for example, if a relative dies.

[2] For three years, a monk undertaking this rite must run 21 miles each day for 100 days. It is not easy because the path is steep, unlit (each run starts at midnight), and he must stop 260 times to pray. The straw sandals he wears offer little protection for his feet and they wear out quite easily. He will go through a couple of pairs on average during each 21-mile run. He is allowed to carry candles for light, some food, and a prayer book. He also carries a knife and rope in case he fails.

[3] In the fourth and fifth years, the monk must run the 21 miles for 200 days straight. Although this is very demanding, the most dangerous part, called the *doiri*, comes after. During the *doiri*, the monk must go without food or water, and cannot sleep for seven days. During this time, the monk must sit upright and recite Buddhist chants, up to 100,000 times a day. If the monk survives, then he is allowed to carry on with the *Kaihogyo*.

[4] In the sixth year, the monk must travel 37.5 miles (60 km) each day for 100 days. Later, in the seventh year, the monk goes 52.5 miles (84 km) for 100 days. During this time, a monk is lucky if he gets a few hours of sleep between runs. Finally, the monk goes back to running 21 miles a day for 100 days. By the time the *Kaihogyo* is over, the monk will have completed 25,800 miles, the equivalent of running around the world.

[5] Only 47 men are recorded as having completed the *Kaihogyo*, although many more have tried. This is probably the most physically and mentally exhausting endurance test in the world. Incredibly, three men have completed the *Kaihogyo* twice.

Word Work

7 **Change the bold word(s) in each sentence with a word chunk from the text.**

a. Before I **begin** my trip to Japan, I need to get my passport renewed.

_____

b. I can't believe that Genshin Fujinami would have to **commit suicide** if he fails.

_____

c. When I train for a marathon, I usually have to buy a few pairs of sneakers because they **fall apart** quickly. _____

d. When you travel in an airplane, you are only **permitted to bring** certain items in your carry-on luggage. _____

e. At times I don't want to **continue** studying because I want to just relax and enjoy life.

_____

Before Reading

1 **What do you think presidents do after they leave office?**
   a. Build houses for the poor.
   b. Sell expensive cars.
   c. Make money for rich people.
   d. Raise awareness of global problems.
   e. Give medicine to the sick.
   f. Provide food for the poor.
   g. Your idea: _____

2 **Read the title of the text on the opposite page. What do you think the text is about?**
   a. The stories of what Nelson Mandela and Jimmy Carter did after they were president.
   b. A comparison of Carter and Mandela's work after being president.
   c. An explanation of how Carter and Mandela each became president.

While Reading

3 While you read the text, annotate it to help you remember significant ideas.

After Reading

4 Discuss the ideas you annotated with a partner.

5 **Highlight the work that:**
   a. Carter did after he was president.
   b. Mandela did after he was president.

6 **These statements describe work that one or both of the presidents did after they were president. Mark each one Carter, Mandela, or Both.**
   a. _____ won the Nobel Peace Prize.
   b. _____ wrote books.
   c. _____ helped children in South Africa.
   d. _____ raised awareness of diseases.
   e. _____ built houses for the poor.

After the Presidency

One of the most important jobs in most countries is the presidency, but it is also one of the most challenging and stressful. When their presidency ends, many former presidents are satisfied [5] with relaxing, writing their memoirs, and giving lectures. However, Jimmy Carter, the former president of the USA, and Nelson Mandela, former president of South Africa, have spent much of their time helping make the world a [10] better place.

Carter was only 56 when he left office in 1981 and although he was not a popular president, he has become widely respected for the work he has done since he left the White House. Besides [15] writing many books and volunteering one week a year to build houses for the poor, his greatest contribution was creating the Carter Center. The Center helps to resolve conflict, promote democracy, protect human rights, reduce poverty, [20] and prevent diseases around the world. In recognition of his work around the world, Carter received the Nobel Peace Prize in 2002.

Like Carter, Mandela also received the Nobel Peace Prize, but he received the award in 1993, [25] before he became president. Mandela was highly admired throughout his time as president from 1994 to 1999 and although Mandela, at 81, was much older than Carter when he left office, he also kept on working to improve people's lives.

[30] Like Carter, Mandela has also written some books, but he spends most of his time on the Nelson Mandela Children's fund. He started this in 1994 to provide better education and health care opportunities to children in South Africa. In [35] addition, he is involved in fighting global diseases. Recently, he has been busy increasing awareness of the HIV/AIDS virus and spends time raising money for the Nelson Mandela Foundation to fight the disease in southern Africa. Even though [40] Mandela is in his nineties, he continues to travel around the world to speak on these issues.

Mandela and Carter are respected internationally for their work. With their knowledge and connections, they could have spent their [45] retirement making money for themselves, but they chose to use their influence to help make the world a better place for everyone.

Word Work

7 Circle the verb which does NOT collocate with the noun in bold.

a. **lectures**:	give	attend	deliver	make
b. **their time**:	give	waste	spend	leave
c. **diseases**:	eliminate	learn	prevent	fight
d. **awareness**:	grow	raise	increase	develop
e. **money**:	spend	raise	develop	make

Reading **3** The Judo Match

Before Reading

1 Look at the title and picture. Tell a partner what you think the text is about.
  a. An interview with someone who studies judo.
  b. A comparison between judo and karate.
  c. An explanation about how to win a judo match.

2 What words do you associate with judo? Write down words you think could appear in the text.

_____ _____ _____ _____

While Reading

3 As you read the text, visualize images in your mind.

4 Highlight the important stages of the story and annotate your thoughts.

After Reading

5 Circle the images you visualized in your mind. Describe them and any others you saw to a partner.

| a short boy | a car accident | a boy with one arm | a boy and his judo master |

6 Ask a partner these questions about the story:
  a. Was the boy crazy or brave to compete in a judo tournament?
  b. If you were the referee, would you have stopped the match?
  c. Should disabled athletes compete with able-bodied athletes?

7 Decide if the statements are true (T) or false (F), according to the story.
  a. T F Larry is the main character of the story.
  b. T F The boy is young, small, and only has one arm.
  c. T F The boy had to win three matches before the championship match.
  d. T F The older boy won the match because he was stronger and more experienced.
  e. T F The younger boy won the match because he knew one of the most difficult moves in judo and he didn't have a left arm.

The Judo Match

Owen Rodgers is not your typical judo champion. The first thing is his age—he is only ten. Then there is his size—he is small for his age. But perhaps the most surprising fact is that Owen [5] has only one arm.

As someone who practices judo, I had to find out how Owen managed to overcome these challenges to become one of the top judo masters in his age group. Luckily for me, Owen [10] agreed to meet in the park and not on the tatami (the judo mat) to share his amazing story.

Owen started off by telling me how he got involved in the sport. When he was eight, he was in a hideous car accident and lost his left [15] arm. After the accident, he could not play his favorite sport, baseball. However, he was an active boy and wanted to do something, so he decided to study judo and began taking lessons from a well-known judo master.

[20] At first, Owen enjoyed the lessons, but he soon noticed that his judo master was only showing him one move. Though Owen kept asking if he should learn some more moves, he said his judo master would always reply, "This is the [25] only move you need to know."

Owen went on to say, "After several months, my judo master entered me into a judo tournament. I easily won the first three matches to make it to the championship round. However, [30] in this round the opponent was a few years older and was much bigger than me. Initially, the older boy seemed to be winning. The audience was becoming worried and thought I was going to get seriously hurt. They started [35] yelling at the referee to stop the match. Right when the referee was about to intervene, my judo master quietly told him not to worry and that I would be fine."

Throughout the match, Owen remained focused, [40] waiting for the opportunity to use his one move. Finally that time came. Owen saw his opportunity and used the move to throw and pin his opponent. Owen was the champion!

Owen recalled how on the drive home, he asked [45] his master how he had won the tournament with only one move. The master replied, "First, you learned one of the most difficult throws in judo. Second, the only known defense of that move is for your opponent to grab your left arm."

[50] As I left my meeting with Owen, I could not help but be inspired by his story of determination and perseverance. He truly is a champion.

Word Work

8 | Use these word chunks to write sentences about yourself or someone you know.

a. small for his/her age: _____
b. take lessons: _____
c. become worried: _____
d. get seriously hurt: _____

Reflection

▶ Which was your favorite text in this unit? Why?

▶ Which reading strategies did you use in this unit?

▶ Which new word chunks will you make an effort to use in the next five days? Choose at least five.

Warm Up

1 Mr. Mystic claims he can read your mind. Follow the instructions and see if he is telling the truth.

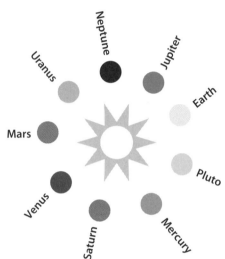

Look at the planets on the right. Choose a planet. Follow these instructions and I will read your mind.

Place your finger on Neptune.

In a clockwise direction around the sun, spell out the name of your planet by moving your finger from one planet to the next, each planet representing a letter. For example, if you are thinking about Mars, you would spell "M" and touch Jupiter, spell "A" and touch Earth, spell "R" and touch Pluto and spell "S" and touch Mercury.

Keep your finger on the planet that you landed on. Spell the name of this new planet. Like before, move a planet at a time in a clockwise direction – one planet for each letter.

Keep your finger on the planet you landed on. Concentrate hard on the name of the planet your finger is touching.

Your finger is touching Earth!

2 Did Mr. Mystic know which planet your finger was touching? Choose another planet and see if the answer is the same.

Reading Strategy: Recognizing main ideas

Any article, essay, formal email, or letter you read has a main idea. The **main idea**, or message, is usually in the first paragraph of the text, and sometimes repeated in the last paragraph as a conclusion.
Each paragraph in that text will also have a main idea. **The main idea of each paragraph** gives more information about **the main message/idea for the text.**

For example, an article about how people fear global warming has that as the main message or idea. While the first paragraph will say people fear global warming, the main ideas in the other paragraphs could be:
Paragraph 2: More people believe global warming is happening.
Paragraph 3: More people are affected by global warming.
Paragraph 4: The effects of global warming are becoming more dangerous.

These main ideas will often be in the first sentence of each paragraph. Sometimes they will be repeated in the last sentence of the paragraph too.

Strategy in Focus

1 | Read the text. Highlight the sentence containing the main idea for the text.

Mind Readers

[1] Magicians or psychics who claim they can read your mind do not have magical powers. However, they are good at understanding and predicting human behavior. A mind reader is very good at asking leading questions—questions that get the listener to think and answer in a predictable way.

[2] One type of leading question is one that only has one or two possible answers. For example, a mind reader might say, "Relax and picture a big European monument—a building or a structure in Europe. Then think of the city that it is in." The mind reader will then say you were thinking of the Eiffel Tower in Paris, and in most cases he or she will be right because there are not that many other options.

[3] A mind reader can ask leading questions about your life in the same way. For example, if you are in your 30s or 40s, he/she will say, "You are going through changes in your life." or "Someone close to you is having health or marital problems." How many people in their 30s and 40s are not going through changes in their life, personally, professionally, or in their family?

[4] Mind readers know what people are feeling and experiencing because most people have similar experiences. They cannot read your mind or know your future but they are good at predicting how you will answer questions.

Feedback:

Answer: The main idea is often found at the end of the first paragraph. In this article, the end of the first paragraph explains that mind readers ask questions most people will answer the same way.

2 | Read the second paragraph. Highlight the sentence containing the main idea for this paragraph.

a. You have to relax before a mind reader can read your mind.

b. Everyone thinks of the Eiffel Tower as a famous monument in Europe.

c. Mind readers ask leading questions with very few possible answers.

3 | Read the third paragraph. Highlight the sentence containing the main idea for this paragraph.

a. Mind readers ask questions about your life with predictable answers.

b. People go to mind readers to find out if they are going to get a divorce.

c. People in their 30s and 40s go through life-changing experiences.

Feedback:

2. = c.; 3. = a. After the first paragraph, the main idea for each paragraph is usually in the first sentence of the paragraph.

Hypnosis: Not Just a Magic Trick

Before Reading

1 Skim the text. Look at the title and picture then read the first and the last sentence of each paragraph. What is the main idea of the text?
  a. Maria Montalvo is scared of hospitals, surgery, and needles.
  b. Hypnosis is becoming more popular to prevent pain during surgery.
  c. Under hypnosis, the patient is relaxed but their subconscious mind stays active.

While Reading

2 Read the text more carefully and check your hypothesis.

After Reading

3 Ask a partner the following questions about the text.
  a. What is the main idea in the text?
  b. What do you think of using hypnotherapy for surgery instead of anesthetic?
  c. Do you think hypnotherapy will become popular in your country?

4 Highlight the sentence(s) containing the main idea for the second paragraph.
  a. Hypnotherapy is a trick.
  b. General anesthesia can be dangerous.
  c. Hypnotherapy is becoming more popular.

5 Highlight the sentence(s) containing the main idea for the fourth paragraph.
  a. Maria felt some pain during the surgery.
  b. Maria preferred hypnotherapy to general anesthesia.
  c. Maria had help from her hypnotherapist before and during surgery.

6 Find these words in the text. What do they refer to?
  a. those (line 3):
     i.   people who prefer hypnotherapy
     ii. people who are scared of operations
     iii. people who suffer from the side effects of using anesthesia
  b. their (line 19):
     i.   doctors   ii. patients   iii. hypnotherapists
  c. them (line 23):
     i.   doctors   ii. hypnotherapists   iii. patients
  d. they (line 35):
     i.   hypnotherapists   ii. patients   iii. doctors

Hypnosis: Not Just a Magic Trick

Many people have a fear of hospitals and they dread operations, and needles. Maria Montalvo was one of those people. She had suffered from the side effects of using anesthetics in
[5] past surgeries, so when she was told that she needed a knee operation, she was naturally scared. However, her anxiety disappeared when her doctor told her of an alternative treatment—hypnotherapy.

[10] Hypnosis, once thought of as just a magician's trick, is becoming more common in hospital operating rooms. Instead of using general anesthetic, a drug which makes the patient unconscious and can have side effects such
[15] as nausea, a few patients are now able to choose to use hypnotherapy as an alternative to anesthetics.

Under hypnotherapy, the patient is in a relaxed state, but their subconscious remains active
[20] and open to suggestions. No general anesthetic is given, instead a trained hypnotherapist makes suggestions to the patient to help them relax and control the pain. Maria had used hypnosis once before to help
[25] her stop smoking so she knew that she would be a good candidate for hypnotherapy.

Although Maria was in control of her hypnotherapy, her hypnotherapist was with her the whole time. A few days before the surgery,

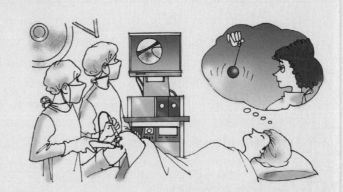

[30] Maria worked with her hypnotherapist to practice self-hypnosis. On the day of the surgery, she hypnotized herself and was brought into the operating room. Maria later described being fully aware of the surroundings; she could hear
[35] the doctors talking and knew when they were operating on her knee, but she could not feel much pain. Throughout the surgery, her hypnotherapist was by her side to make sure Maria did not come out of her hypnosis.

[40] The surgery, which involved drilling her bones, was a success and Maria insists she felt only a small amount of pain. More importantly, after the surgery she had none of the nausea that she had had after past surgeries, and she
[45] quickly recovered from the operation.

Word Work

7 Circle the correct word chunk for each sentence.

a. Sometimes when you take medication, you suffer from **side effects / side affects**.

b. It's **becoming more frequent / becoming more common** for people to have Internet access in their homes.

c. During my grandmother's funeral, I **was on control / was in control** of my emotions until I saw my brother start to cry.

d. When my little sister had to go to the hospital, my mother was **by her side / with her side** the entire time.

e. I only ate **a small amount of / a little amount of** lunch because I had had an enormous breakfast.

Using Your Brain

Before Reading

1 Check [✓] the statements that are true.

a. _____ The main idea is often in the first paragraph of a text.

b. _____ The main idea often adds extra, interesting information about the topic.

c. _____ The main idea is often the last sentence of the first paragraph.

d. _____ The main idea can be repeated in the last paragraph of a text.

e. _____ Each paragraph of a text often has a main idea.

f. _____ The main idea of a paragraph is usually in the middle of the paragraph.

g. _____ The main idea of each paragraph gives more information about the main idea for the text.

2 Take two minutes to skim the text. What is the main idea of the text?

While Reading

3 Circle the images you visualized in your mind while reading the text.

a computer monitor	someone using computer keyboard	a TV remote control
a university building	Mathew Nagel	a scientist in a white coat

After Reading

4 Tell a partner what you saw in your mind as you read the text.

5 What is the main idea in these paragraphs?

Paragraph 2:

a. Matthew Nagle is unable to move his arms and legs.

b. Nagle can play a video game, turn on the TV, and open email.

c. Scientists have developed a micro-chip that can be put into the brain to read your thoughts.

Paragraph 4:

a. The operation to put a micro-chip into someone's brain is risky.

b. Soon you will be able to wear a headband containing a tiny computer.

c. A tiny computer worn in a headband will be able to control planes.

Paragraph 5:

a. This technology is unbelievable.

b. German scientists have invented a device that reads electrical activity in the brain.

c. This technology exists and scientists are working to improve it.

CD 2:
Track 5

Using Your Brain

[1] Imagine a day when you can just think about writing a paper and the words magically appear on the computer screen! How about being able to turn on the TV without pushing a button or using a remote control? Or being able to check your email without touching a keyboard? It may sound like science fiction, but the technology to control machines by just thinking about them is now being developed.

[2] Scientists at Brown University in the United States have developed sophisticated technology that allowed a quadriplegic man to play a video game using his brain like a remote control. Matthew Nagle was able to play simple video games, turn on a TV, and open an email just by using his thoughts even though he was unable to move his arms and legs. Nagle was able to do all of this thanks to a micro-chip in his brain.

[3] For Nagle, the results were amazing, and gave him back some of the independence he lost when he became paralyzed. Although this technology is still being developed, scientists are excited about the future of mind control and computer technology, especially for people who have problems controlling their movements.

[4] Would you want to undergo risky surgery to have a micro-chip put in your brain though? In the future you may not need to. Some scientists think that people will soon be able to wear headbands which contain tiny computers that read their thoughts and allow them to control machines, such as household appliances, cars, and even planes.

[5] This may sound unbelievable, but in fact a scientist in Germany has already invented a device that allows users to send messages and commands to a computer. The device reads electrical activity in a person's brain through the skin on their forehead and communicates their thoughts to a computer. Although the technology is basic at the moment, scientists around the world are working to improve it.

[6] All of this reflects the fact that technology once thought of as futuristic and science-fiction is rapidly becoming a reality. At this rate of technological progress, we may all be wearing headbands and using our thoughts to control machines much sooner than we expect.

Word Work

6 | **Complete the sentences with a word chunk from the text.**

> writing a paper
> at this rate of technological progress
>
> undergo risky surgery
> sooner than we expect
>
> household appliances

a. Life has gotten much easier with the invention of _____ such as the dishwasher and washer dryer.

b. My grandmother has to _____ because she needs a heart transplant.

c. My English assignment involved _____ on the influences of music.

d. Every day, something new is being invented. _____, I think that people will be living on Mars much _____ .

Saving My Sister

Before Reading

1 Read the title and the first paragraph. What is the purpose of the text?

    a. to inform   **b.** to persuade   **c.** to entertain

While Reading

2 Read the text and put the pictures in order. Each picture shows the main idea for each part of the text.

A	B	C	D

After Reading

3 Talk about these questions with a partner.

    a. Did the text make you feel sad / make you laugh / ...?
    b. Did it have an unexpected ending / predictable ending / ...?
    c. Did it sound familiar to you?
    d. Did it remind you of a special connection you have with a friend or sibling?

4 What is the main idea of the text?

    a. Miki and Hiroko can read each other's minds because they are twins.
    b. Hiroko doesn't tell Miki the truth because Miki worries too much about her.
    c. Hiroko and Miki understand they have a strong connection because of the life-saving experience.

5 Who had these experiences? Complete the statements with Miki, Hiroko, or Both.

    a. _____ was concerned that something was wrong with her sister.
    b. _____ often knew what the other sister was thinking and feeling.
    c. _____ was busy with college.
    d. _____ thought her sister was too worried.
    e. _____ enjoyed hanging out with the other one.

CD 2:
Track 6

Saving My Sister
by Miki Nakazawa

My sister, Hiroko, and I have always had a strong connection—the kind where we can almost read each other's minds. A lot of people say it is common for twins to have that [5] connection, but I had never thought about it much. However, I do now as it was our special connection that saved her life last year.

When Hiroko left for college, I was afraid we would not stay in touch, but thanks to instant [10] messaging and cell phones, that didn't happen. I was really looking forward to her coming home during her break, but when she got home, I felt something was wrong.

I asked her if she was feeling okay but she [15] quickly replied that everything was fine. Then I asked her when she had last had a checkup but she just replied, "Sis, I'm fine. You worry about me too much. I'm healthy and happy; I'm just busy with school, that's all."

[20] I dropped the subject as I could tell that she was beginning to get fed up with me. We spent the rest of her vacation hanging out and having fun. However, I had a nagging feeling that something was wrong with her.

[25] A month later, out of the blue, I decided to visit her. As I was driving to her school, I suddenly couldn't breathe. I stopped the car. I thought that I was having an allergic reaction to something, but then I realized that it wasn't [30] something wrong with me; it was with my sister. I quickly called Hiroko to see how she was. She answered the phone and reassured me that things were fine.

About twenty five minutes later, I had another [35] attack, much worse than before and all I could see in my mind were pictures of my sister lying on the floor and gasping for breath. I tried calling her again, but this time she didn't answer. Fearing the worst, I raced to the [40] college, parked the car, and ran to her dorm room.

When I got to her room, it was just like I had seen in my mind. I called an ambulance and they took her to the hospital. The doctor later [45] told me that she had had a severe asthma attack and that if I had arrived a minute or two later, she could have had brain damage or worse!

When my sister woke up, she smiled weakly, [50] and said she would never doubt our special connection again.

Word Work

6 Match the word chunk with its definition.

a. stay in touch •   • i. to remain in communication with someone
b. look forward to •   • ii. to expect something bad
c. be out of the blue •   • iii. to be excited about something
d. fear the worse •   • iv. to be unexpected

Reflection

▶ Which was your favorite text in this unit? Why?

▶ Which reading strategies did you use in this unit?

▶ Which new word chunks will you make an effort to use in the next five days? Choose at least five.

9 Understanding Fear

Warm Up

Take the fear quiz to find out how you cope with fear.

Fear Quiz

1 Standing close to the edge of a balcony:
- **a.** makes you dizzy and frightened.
- **b.** isn't too bad if you don't look down.
- **c.** is no problem.

2 When you see a big spider, you
- **a.** feel very afraid and uncomfortable.
- **b.** leave it alone.
- **c.** let it crawl onto your hand so you can see it better.

3 During a heavy, late-night thunderstorm, you:
- **a.** hide under your covers.
- **b.** sleep—it is only a storm.
- **c.** read a horror story because the storm makes the story scarier.

4 You are at a party and you don't know anyone, so you:
- **a.** sit by yourself and wait for someone to talk to you.
- **b.** look for another person who doesn't know anyone.
- **c.** go up to the first person you see and introduce yourself.

5 The idea of going sky diving:
- **a.** scares you a lot.
- **b.** tempts you but you wouldn't do it alone.
- **c.** excites you—you would love to try it.

6 When you see a dog on the street without a leash, you:
- **a.** get out of there quietly, hoping the dog won't notice you.
- **b.** stick around but keep your distance.
- **c.** find the owner and ask if you can play with the dog.

Fear Quiz Scores: a. = 3 points; b. = 2 points; c. = 1 point
What your total score means:
If you scored 15—18 points, you are easily scared and probably avoid taking risks.
If you scored 10—14 points, you are cautious but willing to take risks and face danger.
If you scored 6—9 points, you have no fear and might even look for dangerous experiences.

Reading Strategy: Recognizing supporting ideas

Each paragraph in the text has usually a main idea and **supporting ideas** that help the reader understand the main idea more clearly. These supporting ideas can be definitions, explanations/descriptions, anecdotes (personal stories), opinions, facts, or examples.

If the main idea for the paragraph is more people should be afraid of global warming, then the supporting ideas would probably give examples of why people should be afraid; for example, floods, hurricanes, droughts, etc.

Strategy in Focus

1 Read the first paragraph. Then highlight the sentence(s) containing the main idea.

Do You Have an Unnatural Fear of Heights?

[1] Fear of heights is a common feeling that is easy to understand. According to many psychologists a fear of heights is one of only two natural fears—the other is fear of loud noises. If you are on the edge of a cliff, it is useful to be a little afraid. If you are not afraid, you could walk too close to the edge and fall off. Having a fear of heights is good because it protects us from real danger.

[2] However, some people have an irrational and unhealthy fear of heights. They experience intense fear even inside a safe environment such as a skyscraper, which is not an appropriate response and it is not helpful. John Adams, an English teacher, has an irrational fear of heights that makes his life very difficult. "As long as I can remember, I have had a powerful fear of heights. It can completely ruin a vacation. For example, when I was with friends in Paris, I became terrified while going up the Eiffel Tower. I was almost crying and I felt embarrassed for the rest of the vacation." Adams recalled.

[3] Fortunately, having an irrational fear of heights can be corrected. There are a number of ways this can be achieved. The most effective seems to be getting the person to acknowledge their fear, for example, by encouraging them to go to the top of tall buildings, hike up steep mountains, or stand on a high bridge. Other ways include hypnosis and acupuncture.

[4] It is important to remember that an inappropriate fear of heights is not unusual and can be treated.

2 Read the second paragraph and check [✓] the main idea. Then highlight the sentence(s) containing the main idea.

a. _____ Fear of heights is irrational.
b. _____ Being afraid in a skyscraper is an irrational fear.
c. _____ An irrational fear of heights can make life difficult.

3 Check [✓] the kinds of supporting ideas in paragraph 2.

a. _____ explanation   **b.** _____ anecdote   **c.** _____ opinion   **d.** _____ facts
e. _____ examples

4 Read the third paragraph and check [✓] the main idea. Then highlight the sentence(s) containing the main idea.

a. _____ An irrational fear of heights can be dangerous.
b. _____ An irrational fear of heights can be cured.
c. _____ An irrational fear is cured by hypnotherapy.

5 Check [✓] the kind of supporting ideas in paragraph 3.

a. _____ explanation   **b.** _____ anecdote   **c.** _____ opinion   **d.** _____ facts
e. _____ examples

Feedback:
Answers = 2. c; 3. a. and b.; 4. b; 5. a. and e.

Phobia: Inside the World of Fear

Before Reading

1 Check [✓] the statements that are true for you. Share your responses with a partner.

I know someone who is afraid of:

_____ heights   _____ thunderstorms   _____ public speaking   _____ spiders   _____ flying

2 Take two minutes to skim the text. What is the main idea of the text?

a. Fears and phobias are caused by psychological traumas.
b. There are millions of people who have fears or phobias.
c. It is possible for people to defeat their fears or phobias.

While Reading

3 Read the article and underline any information that you didn't know before.

After Reading

4 Read the following statements and write (New) if this information is new to you or (Old) if it is something you knew already.

a. _____ Some people are afraid of clowns.
b. _____ A phobia is an irrational fear of something ordinary.
c. _____ A phobia can be caused by psychological trauma.
d. _____ Fear can be useful because it protects us from danger.
e. _____ Cognitive therapy helps people to face their fear.

5 Highlight the sentence(s) containing the main idea in the second paragraph. Then check [✓] the kind of supporting ideas in that paragraph.

a. _____ explanation   b. _____ anecdote   c. _____ opinion   d. _____ facts
e. _____ examples

6 Highlight the sentence(s) containing the main idea in the third paragraph. Then check [✓] the kind of supporting ideas in that paragraph.

a. _____ explanation   b. _____ anecdote   c. _____ opinion   d. _____ facts
e. _____ examples

7 Highlight the sentence(s) containing the main idea in the fourth paragraph. Then check [✓] the kind of supporting ideas in that paragraph.

a. _____ explanation   b. _____ anecdote   c. _____ opinion   d. _____ facts
e. _____ examples

Phobia: Inside the World of Fear

[1] Some people hide in their house every time there is a thunderstorm. Others get goose bumps just thinking of spiders, snakes, or even a clown at a child's birthday party. Millions of people are terrified of ordinary things. These people have phobias which can make their lives very difficult. Why are some people affected by phobias but others are not, and can they be helped?

[2] Fear is useful to protect us, but people with phobias are afraid even when there is no real danger. Their fear is so bad that it stops them from enjoying their lives fully. For instance, someone who is claustrophobic has an unnatural fear of small or tight spaces. They might have difficulty taking an elevator or being in a crowded space like a subway. Other common phobias are mysophobia (fear of germs), aviophobia (fear of flying), and acrophobia (fear of heights). These phobias can severely effect someone's life.

[3] Although fear is not a pleasant experience, it is often useful because it protects us from danger. However, phobics, people who are afraid even when there is no real danger, are not simply afraid; their fear is so bad that it stops them from leading a normal life.

[4] Sarah French was always scared of heights. She felt paralyzed at the top of escalators or long flights of stairs. She explained that she was afraid of falling and could not move her feet. Sarah could not do many everyday things because of her fear of heights. When her son was very young, she could not even play with him on swings or slides. It affected her personality, her confidence, and her family.

[5] Often the person with a fear is not the only person who suffers. Sarah's son Jake remembers one incident, "While going for a walk in the country, we all had to walk across a small, wooden bridge without handrails. We had to crawl across the bridge because my mother thought we might fall off."

[6] However, with the help of a therapist, Sarah fought her phobia. She used an approach called cognitive therapy. To overcome her fear, her therapist helped her to climb a small ladder to show her that she was in control and not in danger. Eventually, Sarah was able to take an elevator to the top of the Empire State Building and look down on New York City.

Word Work

8 Replace the bold word chunks with the words below.

hiking	could not move	whenever	caused by	terrified

a. Some people hide in their house **every time** there is a thunderstorm.

b. Others are **scared to death** of spiders, snakes, or even a clown at a child's birthday party.

c. Some phobias may be **a result of** a psychological trauma, a defect in the brain, or even human evolution.

d. Sarah **felt paralyzed** at the top of escalators or long flights of stairs.

e. Sarah's son remembers **going for a walk** in a park where the family had to walk across a small, wooden bridge without handrails.

Beat Your Fears and Phobias

Before Reading

1 Take two minutes to skim the text. Read the title as well as the first and last paragraph. What is the main idea?

    a. An explanation of how difficult it is to overcome fears.
    b. A description of how professionals help to overcome fears.
    c. An explanation of different strategies and techniques to beat fears.

While Reading

2 As you read the text, annotate it to help you remember significant ideas.

After Reading

3 Read the second paragraph. Choose the main idea for this paragraph. Then highlight the sentence(s) containing the main idea.

    a. Learning more about your fears can help to beat the problem.
    b. Studying about the fear on the Internet is the best way to become an expert.
    c. There are classes that teach doctors how to treat fears.

4 Check [✓] the kind of supporting ideas in the second paragraph.

    a. _____ explanation   **b.** _____ anecdote   **c.** _____ opinion   **d.** _____ facts
    e. _____ examples

5 Read the third paragraph. Choose the main idea for this paragraph. Then highlight the sentence(s) containing the main idea.

    a. There are professionals who can train people to eat well and exercise properly.
    b. Eating healthy foods instead of fast food will help beat fears.
    c. Living a healthy life will help beat fears by reducing anxiety and increasing energy.

6 Check [✓] the kind of supporting ideas in the third paragraph.

    a. _____ explanation   **b.** _____ anecdote   **c.** _____ opinion   **d.** _____ facts
    e. _____ examples

7 Decide if the bold statements in the text are fact (F) or opinion (O), according to the writer.

    a. _____   **b.** _____   **c.** _____   **d.** _____   **e.** _____   **f.** _____

Beat Your Fears and Phobias

[1] How can you overcome your fears? You can find someone to help you, or you could make some simple changes to your life on your own. (a) **Trying to help yourself is difficult** but it is possible if you follow certain strategies and techniques.

[2] There are a number of things you can do to beat your fears. (b) **One important strategy is to become an expert in your problem.** There are countless books and websites providing up-to-date theories and explanations about phobias. You can also go to lectures and workshops. If you become an expert in your phobia, you will be able to make good decisions about the best treatment to overcome it.

[3] (c) **A simple way to beat your phobia on your own is to maintain a healthy lifestyle.** A healthy lifestyle will make it easier for you to live with the anxiety. Getting regular exercise can help you feel less anxious and will give you more energy. Eating well-balanced meals can have the same effect. Not eating properly will decrease your energy level and can increase anxiety and depression. Reducing the amount of coffee you drink and getting plenty of sleep will also help reduce anxiety and increase energy.

[4] However, for many fears these simple lifestyle changes may not be enough. You may consider professional help, such as from doctors or psychologists. They may recommend one of the many kinds of alternative therapy. There are a number of techniques an alternative therapist might use, some of which are briefly described below.

Hypnosis: In hypnosis, a professional puts the patient into a sleep-like state. While hypnotized the patient is told that their fears will disappear when they wake up.

[5] Emotional Freedom Technique (EFT): (d) **EFT relieves fear by rubbing and tapping eight different spots on the body, located on the head, the face, and the chest.** Patients begin by rubbing on one spot and repeating a statement for example, "Even though I have a fear of heights, I accept myself." (e) **Then they tap on each of the spots about seven times while thinking about their fear.**

[6] Art Therapy: (f) **Drawing, painting, and sculpting help many people to resolve problems, express emotions, and encourage self-awareness.**

[7] Do not feel overwhelmed by the advice in this leaflet. If you feel your fears are too big to beat on your own, and you are not sure what to do, do not be afraid to talk to your doctor.

Word Work

8 Change the bold words in the sentence with a word chunk from the text.

a. I don't mind traveling **by myself**, but I prefer traveling with friends. _____

b. I love wearing the most **current** fashions, but it is expensive to buy new clothes every season.

_____

c. I'm determined to get in shape so I'm exercising and eating **nutritious meals**.

_____

d. Like many people, I went to a therapist to help **settle issues** that I have had since I was a child.

_____

e. If you are **not certain** about where to go on vacation, you should talk to a travel agent.

_____

The Babysitter

Before Reading

1 **Ask a partner these questions.**

   a. Have you ever been a babysitter?
   b. Have you ever been frightened when alone in a house?
   c. How would you feel if you received a prank call? What would you do?

While Reading

2 **Read the story and put the pictures in order. Each picture shows an important part of the story.**

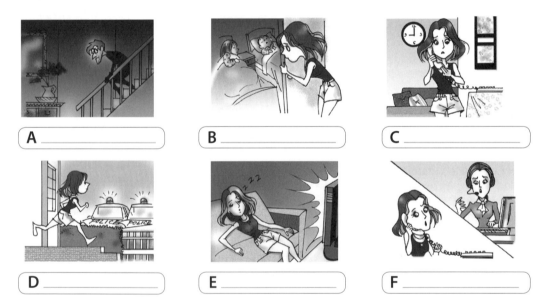

A _____   B _____   C _____

D _____   E _____   F _____

After Reading

3 **With a partner, complete these sentences about the story.**

   a. I think the story is ...   **b.** I like ...   **c.** I don't like ...
   d. I felt ...   **e.** The babysitter ...

4 **Find the words below in the reading. Then match each word with its synonym by deducing its meaning from context.**

   a. exhausted (line 2)   •   •   **i.**   to insert / put inside
   b. popped in (line 7)   •   •   **ii.** to fall asleep
   c. dozed off (line 13)   •   •   **iii.** not anxious anymore
   d. to trace (line 42)   •   •   **iv.** very tired
   e. relieved (line 53)   •   •   **v.**   to find the location of something

The Babysitter

It was eight o'clock in the evening and Meghan was exhausted. She had spent the day babysitting the Potter children, ages 4 and 6, and was glad that they had finally fallen asleep.
[5] Now, all she had to do was wait a few more hours until the children's parents came home. She had just popped in a movie and settled down on the couch when the phone rang.

"Hello, Potter residence," she answered.

[10] She waited for a reply but nobody answered. "Must be a wrong number," she thought as she hung up the phone. She sat back down to watch the movie. During the movie she dozed off.

An hour later, the phone rang again. The ringing
[15] jolted Meghan awake. As she answered the phone she tried to shake the sleepiness from her voice.

"Hello, Potter house," she said. On the other end, a man was laughing hysterically.

[20] "Who is this?" Meghan asked, but the man just continued laughing. She quickly hung up.

Meghan had gotten prank calls before so she was not really scared; she figured that a friend was just playing a joke on her. But just as a
[25] precaution she decided to lock the doors.

At ten o'clock, the phone rang again. She picked up the phone, but this time the caller said, "One more hour," and hung up. Meghan was starting to get a little nervous. She decided to check on
[30] the kids to make sure that the phone had not woken them up. As she went up to their bedrooms, she switched on all the lights. She found both children sleeping peacefully and went back downstairs.

[35] Half and hour later the phone rang again. Meghan thought about not answering it, but realizing it could be the Potters, she picked it up. "You'll see me real soon," the man said quietly before he hung up. Now, Meghan was
[40] both scared and irritated.

She decided to call the operator to complain and ask them to trace the call. The operator agreed, and said it would take a minute and she would call back. A minute passed and the
[45] phone rang. It was the operator telling her that the call was coming from inside the house. She said she would call the police, but advised Meghan to get out of the house as quickly as she could.

[50] Just then Meghan heard a door open upstairs. A man she had never seen before started walking down the stairs towards her. As Meghan raced out of the house, she was relieved to see two police cars coming up the driveway.

Word Work

5 Use these word chunks to write sentences about yourself.

a. spent the day: _____
b. a wrong number: _____
c. dozed off: _____
d. had never seen before: _____

Reflection

▶ Which was your favorite text in this unit? Why?

▶ Which reading strategies did you use in this unit?

▶ Which new word chunks will you make an effort to use in the next five days? Choose at least five.

Review Reading Strategies

- Unit 7: Highlighting and annotating
- Unit 8: Recognizing the main ideas
- Unit 9: Recognizing supporting ideas

1 Read each statement and write the reading strategy that is being described.

	Reading Strategy
a. The most important message of a paragraph.	
b. To write brief notes next to a text to help you find important information.	
c. Develops the main idea of a paragraph.	
d. The most important message of the whole text.	
e. Marking key words in a text to help you remember and find important ideas.	
f. Develops the main idea of the text.	

2 Read the first paragraph of the text. Choose the main idea. Underline the sentence(s) containing the main idea.

a. Air travel is much more comfortable today than in 1903.
b. The Wright brothers were the first people to successfully fly an airplane.
c. Airplane flight depends upon four forces.

3 Highlight the key idea in each paragraph.

4 Match the annotation to the paragraph.

	Paragraph				
a. this is similar to how cars are designed, too	1	2	3	4	5
b. take-off = thrust > drag, lift > weight	1	2	3	4	5
c. Humans have been flying in airplanes for over 100 years!	1	2	3	4	5
d. landing = drag > thrust, weight > lift	1	2	3	4	5
e. wing's design (airfoil) essential to flight	1	2	3	4	5

5 Check [✓] the kind of supporting ideas in the third paragraph.

a. _____ explanation   **b.** _____ anecdote   **c.** _____ opinion   **d.** _____ facts
e. _____ examples

6 Check [✓] the kind of supporting ideas in the fourth paragraph.

a. _____ explanation   **b.** _____ anecdote   **c.** _____ opinion   **d.** _____ facts
e. _____ examples

Reading

The Four Principles of Flight

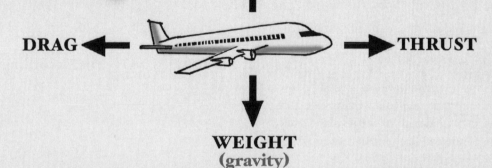

LIFT

DRAG ← → THRUST

WEIGHT
(gravity)

[1] Airplane design has come a long way since the Wright brothers achieved the first, sustained, controlled power flight in 1903, but the basic principles of flight have remained the same. These principles are based on four forces: lift, weight, thrust, and drag.

[2] But in simple terms, how do these forces work to put and keep a plane in the air? First of all, in order for an airplane to ascend into the air, the thrust (engine power and forward force) must be greater than the drag (resistance of air and backward force), and the lift (upward force) must be greater than weight (gravity and downward force).

[3] After takeoff, the key to sustained flight is the shape of the airplane's wing. Called an airfoil, the top of the wing is more curved than the bottom. Because of this design, when a plane is flying, air flows faster over the top of the wing and this results in lower air pressure above the wing. Meanwhile, the slower moving air passing below the wing, which has a higher air pressure, is being pushed downward, which creates the lift. This lift counters the airplane's immense weight.

[4] At the same time, the airplane's engine provides the thrust that keeps the air moving over and under the wing, allowing the plane to remain in the air. Without this thrust, the plane would start to descend. In order to keep the plane moving forward in the air, the thrust must be bigger than the plane's drag. Drag is a mechanical force, as opposed to the natural force of gravity, which is caused by the interaction of the airplane with the air. This interaction causes friction which slows down the plane's forward movement. In order to lessen the drag, most airplanes are designed to be streamlined, which causes less resistance to the air and makes it easier for the plane to keep moving forward. This also explains why in most airplanes, the wheels are retracted after take-off. The pilot wants to create the least amount of resistance to the air.

[5] After the pilot has achieved the desired elevation, or height, he or she then needs to adjust lift and thrust so that they are equal to weight and drag. Doing so will keep the airplane at the same height and speed for the duration of the flight. When it is time to descend, the pilot must again change the relationship between these four forces. Finally, to prepare for landing, the weight must exceed lift, so the plane loses elevation, and the drag must exceed thrust, so that it slows down.

Comprehension Check

1 The word "ascend" in the passage is closest in meaning to:

    a. survive   **b.** climb   **c.** move   **d.** fly

2 The word "retracted" in the passage is closest in meaning to:

    a. taken away   **b.** replaced   **c.** recovered   **d.** pulled in

3 Retracting the airplane's wheels is an example of why a streamlined design is important to lessen the force of:

    a. lift   **b.** thrust   **c.** drag   **d.** weight

4 In the fifth paragraph, the word "they" refers to:

    a. weight and drag   **b.** lift and thrust   **c.** lift and weight   **d.** thrust and drag

5 Which of the following statements about the airfoil is NOT true, according to the text?

    a. It helps to create lower air pressure above the wing.
    b. Without it, an airplane wouldn't be able to fly.
    c. It is also the design of the airplane's tail.
    d. It is connected to the principal of lift.

More Word Chunks

1 Use these word chunks to write sentences about yourself or flying.

    a. a long way: _____
    b. in order to: _____
    c. after / before take-off: _____
    d. slow down: _____

2 Match the word chunk from the text with its definition. Then choose one word chunk and write a sentence about yourself or someone you know.

    a. out of the blue   •   •   **i.** to commit suicide
    b. scared to death   •   •   **ii.** to continue doing something
    c. to carry on   •   •   **iii.** from an unexpected source
    d. to doze off   •   •   **iv.** to be very frightened
    e. to take their own life   •   •   **v.** to fall asleep

3 In Unit 7, we learned about the word chunk "make money."

I made money buying and selling stocks on Wall Street.

Here are some other word chunks with "make" and their definitions:

make do (use whatever you can)
make a killing (earn a lot of money)
make a scene (to complain loudly)
make believe (to imagine, pretend)
make room (to create a space)
make up (to be a friends again)
make it (to go/come/attend)

Complete the sentences with a word chunk from above. Change the verb tense when necessary.

a. Young children have very active imaginations and like to play _____ .

b. When the airplane flight was cancelled, a lot of upset passengers started to _____.

c. There wasn't much room on the bus, so I _____ for an elderly person by putting my bag under the seat rather than on the empty seat next to me.

d. I am going to try to _____ to my friend's party but it starts when I am at work.

e. The business tycoon Donald Trump _____ on selling real estate in the United States.

f. I had a terrible argument with my best friend, but I want to _____ so I think I will apologize to him.

10 Making Mistakes

Warm Up

1 Look at these numbers for 30 seconds. Close your book and on a piece of paper, write down the numbers from memory.

a. 2468 13579

b. 160719651

c. 4321 9876

2 Tell a partner which number(s) you remembered. If you didn't remember all three sets of numbers, tell your partner why you think you remembered some but not others.

Reading Strategy: Recognizing text organization—time order and process

Organization and patterns help us understand and remember things more easily, like the numbers in the warm up. Texts also have organization and patterns that help us understand how a writer has organized their thoughts and ideas.

Some different ways to organize a text are:

- Time Order or Process (Unit 10)
- Compare and Contrast (Unit 11)
- Cause and Effect (Unit 12)

Time Order—Writers usually tell a story or explain events in the order they happen. For example, "This morning, I woke up at 7 a.m. Then I brushed my teeth, showered, dressed, and had breakfast. From 9 a.m. to 4 p.m., I was in school..."

Words often used in time order patterns include: dates, "before," "after," "while," "then," "next," "today," "the next day," "after that," and "when."

Process—Writers usually use process organization when describing how to do something or how something works.

Words commonly used in a process include: "first," "one," "second," "next," "before," "after," "later," "while," "when," "finally," "afterwards," "initially," "in the meantime," "at the same time," and "then."

Feedback to Warm Up:
For most people, b. is the most difficult number to remember, because it does not follow a pattern or any organization.

Strategy in Focus

1 Read the texts to identify their organization – time order (TO) or process (P).

a. _____ Making an Emergency Call   b. _____ Getting Help from Your Friends

Making an Emergency Call

Many visitors to the USA get into dangerous situations because they may not be sure how to call the emergency services. The first thing to do is dial 911. When the operator answers, he or she will first ask you which emergency service you need: police, fire, or medical. Next, the operator will ask for your name and where you are calling from. Finally, you will be asked to describe the emergency and how serious it is. Knowing these steps could avoid making a bad situation worse.

Getting Help from Your Friends

In the fall term of the freshman year of high school in 2006, I had my first experience of bullying. Before class on the first day of school, a boy in my grade started pushing me around in the playground. I was scared and confused but did not tell anybody. The next day, the same thing happened. By the end of the term, the boy had started taking my lunch money. After the fall term finished, I finally talked to my best friend, Barry, about the bullying. After that, Barry's brother, a senior, spoke to the bully and the next term the bully left me alone completely. I should have spoken to Barry earlier.

Feedback:

The first text explains how to make an emergency call. Process organization is used to explain how something is done.

The second text tells the story from start to finish. We learn when the bullying started, how it continued, and how it ended.

2 Write down the words from each text that show its text organization.

a. time order: _____ _____ _____ _____

_____ _____ _____ _____

b. process: _____ _____ _____ _____

_____ _____ _____ _____

Before Reading

1 Quickly scan the text to identify its organization. Check [✓] the correct box below. Underline the words that support your answer.

☐ Time Order   ☐ Process

2 Take a minute to skim the text. What is the main idea?

a. The life of Harry Potter's mother.
b. The woman who wrote the Harry Potter novels.
c. The success of the Harry Potter novels.

3 Read the beginning of the text below. Predict the next words.

J.K. Rowling probably never imagined that she would be one of the richest women in the world, especially when publisher after publisher rejected her first Harry Potter story. No doubt, those same publishers now regret their mistake as the Harry Potter books sold more than …

4 Guess if these statements are true. Write true (T) or false (F).

a. _____ It was easy to find a publisher for Harry Potter.
b. _____ J.K. Rowling had a lot of money before writing Harry Potter.
c. _____ J.K. Rowling is the richest author in the world.

While Reading

5 Read the text and check your hypotheses and prediction.

After Reading

6 Complete the timeline for these events in the correct order.

a. 1965: Rowling born
b. moved to Wales
c. graduated top of her class
d. _____
e. 1986: _____
f. _____
g. taught in Portugal
h. _____
i. moved to Scotland
j. 1997: _____

7 Find the underlined words in the text. Deduce the meaning of each word from its context. Then circle its synonym.

a. The publishers who <u>rejected</u> Harry Potter **didn't read it / didn't want it**.
b. The publishers who <u>regret</u> rejecting Harry Potter think they **made a mistake / were correct**.
c. <u>Convinced</u> means **persuaded / lied**.
d. If you <u>can't afford</u> heat, you don't **have the correct equipment / have enough money**.
e. The agent who <u>represents</u> J.K. Rowling **speaks for her / designs the book for her**.

Harry Potter's Mother

J.K. Rowling probably never imagined that she would be one of the richest women in the world, especially when publisher after publisher rejected her first Harry Potter story. No doubt, those same [5] publishers now regret their mistake as the Harry Potter books sold more than 325 million copies around the world in just over nine years.

Rowling, born in 1965 on July 31st (the same day she chose as Harry Potter's birthday), was [10] born in England. During her childhood, she moved around, eventually ending up living in the countryside near Wales. Rowling enjoyed reading and started writing her own stories when she was around six. She was a good student, [15] especially in languages, and she graduated as the top girl in her class.

Although interested in English literature, her parents convinced her to study something more "useful" at university, so she studied French. After graduating [20] in 1986, she worked as a secretary. She found secretarial work boring though and looked for something more creative and exciting.

That something turned out to be teaching English. When she was 26, Rowling moved to Portugal [25] and began teaching in a language school. It was there she began writing her story about a boy wizard.

While in Portugal, she met and married a Portuguese television journalist. She gave birth to her daughter, [30] Jessica, in 1993. The marriage did not last and Rowling and her daughter went to Scotland to live close to her younger sister, Di.

Life was not easy for Rowling. At times, she had so little money that she did her writing in a cafe [35] because she could not afford to heat her apartment. She had to borrow money from friends. Even after the first book was finished, Rowling struggled to find an agent to represent her to publishers.

[40] Finally, in 1997, a publisher, Bloomsbury, decided to take a chance on the new author and her wizard story. The book became an instant success, and Rowling is now making more money than any other writer.

Word Work

8 Complete the sentences with a word chunk from the text. Change the tense if necessary.

| in just over | end up in | borrow money | take a chance on | an instant success |

a. Few publishers want to _____ a new author because they don't know if their stories will be popular and sell.

b. The tickets for her concert sold out _____ five hours.

c. *Hancock* was _____ . In its opening weekend, it made over 66 million dollars.

d. We took the wrong bus and _____ the wrong part of town.

e. In order to buy a car, I had to _____ from my parents.

What Are You Waiting For?

Before Reading

1 Quickly skim the text. Look at the title and read the first and the last sentence of each paragraph. What is the main idea?

   a. A story about a student called Emily Regan.
   b. A story about people who don't know what they are waiting for.
   c. An explanation about how students can stop wasting time when there is work to finish.

2 Take one minute to scan the text to identify its organization. Check [✓] the correct box below. Underline any words that support your answer.

   ☐ time order   ☐ process

While Reading

3 As you read, decide if the ideas in the text can help you study better.

After Reading

4 Tell a partner if you agree or disagree with these statements.

   a. The text can help me.
   b. I will try some of the ideas for my next homework assignment.
   c. I already use the ideas in the text.
   d. I tend to procrastinate when I have homework.

5 Complete the process chart to help students work better.

   a. stop delaying homework
   b. work a little everyday
   c. _____
   d. _____

6 Choose the best ending to the summary.

   The article *What Are You Waiting For?* explains how students can stop wasting time when they have homework assignments. It ...

   a. describes how a student called Emily Regan spends her time watching television and socializing with her friends instead of doing homework. The article says she should stop doing those things.
   b. explains how students wait to do their homework until the last minute. The author describes how organizing assignments into small pieces, organizing time, and finding a good place to work will help students do their work on time and feel good.
   c. explains that students who work for half an hour a day and don't check their email can work better and do their homework on time. It tells students to do their work in a quiet room so they have less stress.

What Are You Waiting For?

It is the night before the research paper is due, and Emily Regan knows that she will be up all night. She still has to research and write the 10-page paper. Emily's problem is procrastination. [5] She has waited to do her work until the very last second and now she is stressed and has to work through the night to complete her paper. Procrastination is a problem for many students, but it does not have to be. Instead of waiting to [10] start your homework until just before the deadline, you can follow these simple steps.

First, do a little bit every day rather than all at once. For instance, in Emily's case, she could have spent 30 minutes a day working on that [15] research paper and divided her work into sections. One week could have been spent doing research, one week writing an outline, one week writing the first draft, and the final week could have been spent revising and [20] finalizing the paper.

Schedule that study time into your daily activities. Treat your work like any other commitments you have, like classes, extracurricular activities, or a job. Remember, you are the boss and it is [25] up to you to follow your schedule. Be disciplined and do not make any other plans during the time you have set aside that will prevent you from doing your work.

Once you have organized your time in this way, [30] it is important to find a place to work where there are few distractions. For instance, if you are writing a paper, do not go on the Internet to check your email or see who else is online, and do not have a TV in the room. Instead, focus [35] on the work you planned for that time. Afterwards, you can reward yourself for your hard work by doing whatever you want—emailing, socializing with friends, or watching television. You will probably enjoy yourself more because you will [40] not have the work hanging over your head and stressing you out.

Although procrastination is a common mistake that many students make, do not put yourself in Emily's shoes and leave work until the last minute. [45] It is easy to make some simple changes in the way you work to prevent it from happening.

Word Work

7 Match the words to make word chunks from the text. Then choose one word chunk and write a sentence about yourself or someone you know.

a.	the night	•	• **i.**	up all night
b.	be	•	• **ii.**	yourself in (someone's) shoes
c.	work	•	• **iii.**	through the night
d.	hanging	•	• **iv.**	before
e.	put	•	• **v.**	over your head

Before Reading

1 Take one minute to scan the text to identify its organization. Check [✓] the correct box below. Underline any words that support your answer.

☐ time order   ☐ process

While Reading

2 As you read the text, number the pictures in the correct order.

A _____   B _____   C _____

D _____   E _____   F _____

After Reading

3 Check your picture order with a partner.

4 What do the underlined words in these sentences refer to?

a. The friend was known for being very positive, and had the habit of looking at every situation (good and bad) and remarking, "<u>This</u> is good!" (line 3)

_____

b. He was usually very careful with his preparations, but somehow he must have made a mistake because later, when the king fired the gun, <u>his</u> thumb was accidentally blown off. (line 8)

_____

c. He immediately replied, "No, <u>this</u> is NOT good! You made a huge mistake and now you're going to pay for it!" and he sent the friend to jail. (line 20)

_____

d. While they were tying him up in preparation for cooking <u>him</u>, they noticed the king was missing a thumb.(line 30)

_____

e. It was wrong of <u>me</u> to do <u>this</u>. (line 48)

_____

f. If I had NOT been in jail, <u>I</u> would have been on that island with <u>you</u>. (line 54)

_____

This is Good!

One day, a king was out hunting with his usual hunting companion, a close childhood friend. The friend was known for being very positive, and had the habit of looking at every situation [5] (good and bad) and remarking, "This is good!"

That morning, the friend had been responsible for loading and preparing the hunting rifle that the king used. He was usually very careful with his preparations, but somehow he must have [10] made a mistake because later, when the king fired the gun, his thumb was accidentally blown off.

The friend quickly bandaged the hand and made sure the king was going to live. After he realized [15] that the king was OK, the friend remarked as usual, "This is good!" adding, "You've only lost a thumb. You'll heal quickly and be hunting again in no time."

The king could not believe his friend could be [20] so positive in this situation. He immediately replied, "No, this is NOT good! You made a huge mistake and now you're going to pay for it!" and he sent the friend to jail.

About a year later, the king set off by himself on [25] another hunting trip on a small exotic island. The king did not realize that the people living on this island captured and ate any strangers who wandered into their territory. The king was promptly captured and taken to the cannibals' [30] village. While they were tying him up in preparation for cooking him, they noticed the king was missing a thumb. Luckily for the king, the cannibals had a superstition that it was bad luck to eat anyone who was not completely whole, [35] so they untied the king and set him free.

The king could not believe his luck and realized that his old friend's mistake had in fact saved his life. He immediately felt sorry for how he treated his friend and upon returning to his country, went [40] straight to the jail. He wanted to release his friend and apologize for imprisoning him.

Once he got to the jail, he went to his friend and said "You were right. Even though I thought you were crazy for saying it at the time, it was good [45] that my thumb was blown off."

The king told his friend the story about what happened on the island. "I'm very sorry for sending you to jail for so long. It was wrong of me to do this."

[50] "No," his friend replied, "This is good!"

"What do you mean, 'This is good'? How could it be good that I sent my friend to jail for a year?"

"If I had NOT been in jail, I would have been on [55] that island with you." replied the friend.

Word Work

5 | Use these word chunks to write sentences about yourself.

a. a close childhood friend: _____

b. made a mistake: _____

c. couldn't believe: _____

d. felt sorry for (someone): _____

Reflection

▶ Which was your favorite text in this unit? Why?

▶ Which reading strategies did you use in this unit?

▶ Which new word chunks will you make an effort to use in the next five days? Choose at least five.

Warm Up

Who has helped you in your life? Check [✓] the options and discuss with a partner.

a. _____ parents

b. _____ brother or sister

c. _____ friend

d. _____ partner

e. _____ stranger

f. _____ teacher

g. _____ doctor

h. _____ teammates

i. _____ police officer

Reading Strategy: Recognizing text organization–compare and contrast

Writers often use a **compare and contrast** structure when writing about two similar but different things. It is easier to understand two separate things by describing their similarities and differences. In describing America and Japan, for example, the writer might explain the holidays, the food, and the weather in each country. There are two ways the writer can do this:

Block organization—one section about holidays, food, and weather in America, then another about holidays, food, and weather in Japan.

Point by point organization—one paragraph comparing holidays in America with those in Japan, another paragraph comparing food in America with Japanese food, then a final paragraph comparing the weather in America with the weather in Japan.

Words commonly used in a compare and contrast text include: "both," "similar," "same," "also," "alike," "different," "unlike," "more than," "less than," "but," "although," and "however."

Strategy in Focus

1 Skim each text and identify their organization. Write (B) for block organization and (P) for point by point.

a. _____

Seeing a Psychologist

Many of my friends in New York see a psychologist to help them with their problems because it is better than talking to friends. Even though both psychologists and good friends can listen to you talk about your problems, they say psychologists are more objective. For example, a friend may tell you to leave your boyfriend because she doesn't like him, and not because that is the best thing for you. Unlike friends, psychologists are trained to ask the right questions and find the real cause of your problems.

b. _____

Learning a Foreign Language

There are advantages to studying a foreign language in a classroom, but there are also advantages to studying on your own. In a classroom, you have a teacher to help you learn and you can practice with other students. On the other hand, learning on your own allows you to study when it is convenient for you and it is also cheaper than paying for a class or a teacher. If you have the time and money, you should try studying both in class and on your own.

c. _____

English RULES!!!

British and American people both speak the same language, English. However, there are differences in vocabulary, spelling, and grammar, which can cause some problems in understanding. For instance, an American would say, "I had to rent a truck to bring my furniture to my new apartment," while a British person would say, "I had to hire a lorry to take my furniture to my new flat." Obviously, vocabulary can be very different between the two. Another difference is with spelling. Some word endings in American-English, like color, humor, and neighbor, include a "u" in British-English (colour, humour, neighbour). Also, the British do not use "a" and "the" with certain nouns, like university and hospital. They would say, "I went to university," whereas an American would say, "I went to a university."

2 Complete the outline for each text. Compare your answers with a partner.

a. Seeing a Psychologist

    i. help from friends or _____   ii. psychologists more objective

    iii. _____   iv. _____

b. Learning a Foreign Language

    i. studying in class or _____   ii. in class: _____ and practice

    iii. alone: _____ and _____   iv. _____

c. American English RULES!!!

    i. differences in _____ and   ii. differences in _____
    American English

    iii. _____   iv. _____

Feedback to activity 1:

a. P, b. B, c. P

The Rubin "Hurricane" Carter Story

Before Reading

1 Take one minute to skim the text. Look at the title and the picture, then read the first and the last sentence of each paragraph. What is the main idea?

   a. Both Rubin Carter and John Artis were victims of racial discrimination.
   b. The movie, *The Hurricane*, proves Rubin Carter and John Artis are innocent.
   c. Some people think Rubin Carter and John Artis are innocent, but others think they are guilty.

While Reading

2 As you read, decide if the text uses point by point or block text organization. Underline any words that indicate the organization type.

After Reading

3 As you read each paragraph, decide if you agree [✓] or disagree [×] with these judgments.

Paragraph 1:
   a. _____ All murderers lie and say they are innocent.
   b. _____ The movie must be telling the truth.
Paragraph 2:
   a. _____ The police wouldn't have stopped Carter and Artis without a good reason.
   b. _____ The police racially discriminated against Carter and Artis.
Paragraph 3:
   a. _____ Carter had a history of violence. He must have been guilty.
   b. _____ If the witnesses identified Carter and Artis, they must be guilty.
Paragraph 4:
   a. _____ The police stopped Carter and Artis' car for no good reason.
   b. _____ There were no good witnesses to the murders.
Paragraph 5:
   a. _____ Movies are good for learning about history or real events.
   b. _____ Websites are good for learning about history or real events.

4 Complete the outline of the text.

Guilty	vs.	Innocent
i. Carter violent person		**i.** no good evidence for this
ii. _____		**ii.** _____
iii. _____		**iii.** _____

5 Decide if the statements are true (T) or false (F).
   a. T   F   Carter and Artis were found guilty of the murder of three men and a woman.
   b. T   F   A movie about Rubin Carter and the murders came out in 1985.
   c. T   F   On June 17, 1966 there were murders in two different bars in New Jersey.
   d. T   F   No witnesses identified Carter and Artis immediately after the murders.

The Rubin "Hurricane" Carter Story

[1] In 1967, Rubin Carter, a famous boxer, and John Artis, an unemployed teenager, were sentenced to life in jail for the murder a year earlier of two men and a woman. Carter and Artis repeatedly said they were innocent, and in 1985 a court dropped the charges against them and let the men go free. To this day, their innocence is debated. In 1999, a movie called *The Hurricane* told their story, demonstrating their innocence, but there are a number of people who disagree with the movie and argue on websites that the two men are guilty.

[2] Both sides agree that early in the morning of June 17, 1966 two men walked into a bar in New Jersey and shot four people. Two men died instantly and one woman died about a month later in the hospital. The fourth person survived. Witnesses saw two black men in a white car driving away from the scene. A few minutes after the shooting, the police stopped Carter and Artis in a car matching the description. For some people, Carter and Artis are the murderers, but for others they were innocent victims of racial discrimination.

[3] Those who believe Carter and Artis are guilty say Carter had a history of violence and point out that he had a criminal record. They also say he wanted to get revenge for the shooting of a black bar owner by white men earlier that day. Their strongest reason for believing that Carter and Artis are guilty is that the police found two witnesses who identified them as the murderers.

[4] Conversely, those who think Carter and Artis are innocent say the police only stopped their car because the two men are black. There was no firm evidence, such as fingerprints, that connected them to the murders. Second, in the days immediately following the murders, the female survivor did not identify either Carter or Artis as the murderers. Although police found witnesses much later who would identify Carter and Artis, they say these witnesses were convicted criminals who were pressured by the police to lie about what had happened.

[5] If you watch the movie, you will probably believe Carter and Artis are innocent, but if you read some of the websites about the murder trial, you could be convinced they are guilty.

Word Work

6 Spot the differences. Underline any word chunks that are different from the original text. There are five differences.

Witnesses saw two African Americans in a white car leaving the area. Soon after the shooting, the police stopped Carter and Artis in a car resembling the account. For some people, Carter and Artis are the murderers, but for others they were innocent victims of racism.

When in Rome

Before Reading

1 Quickly skim the text. Look at the title and read the first and the last sentence of each paragraph. What is the main idea?

a. A story about a vacation in Rome.
b. Cultural mistakes in Korea and Saudi Arabia.
c. Different types of cultural mistakes people make.

2 Take one minute to scan the text to identify its organization. Check [✓] the correct box below. Underline the words that support your answer.

☐ block organization ☐ point by point organization

While Reading

3 As you read the text, visualize images in your mind.

After Reading

4 Circle any of the following images you visualized. Describe them and any others you saw to a partner.

| a guest in someone's house | a foreign trip | wearing shoes at home |
| a strange meal | a foreigner you met | an embarrassing mistake |

5 Complete the outline of the text.

a. differences in culture
b. differences in _____
c. _____
d. _____
e. Conclusion: _____

6 Check [✓] the inferences you can make about the text.

a. _____ In some cultures, it is acceptable to wear shoes inside the house.
b. _____ In some cultures, guests should bring food or drink for the host.
c. _____ In Ella Yao's culture, you shouldn't talk while eating.
d. _____ Elizabeth insulted a server in Thailand.
e. _____ Business relationships in the United States are less formal than in Asia.
f. _____ A business can lose a lot of money if its workers make cultural mistakes in Asia.

CD 2:
Track 15

When in Rome

In Korea, it is rude to wear shoes inside someone's house because it is considered dirty. In Saudi Arabia, you would not bring food to someone's house because taking food or drink suggests [5] that you think the host cannot afford the meal. More and more people around the world are traveling abroad to study, to go on vacation, or to work, and while it can be a great way to learn about other cultures, there may be times when [10] travelers accidentally offend their hosts' culture. Before you set off on a trip, it is best to get some helpful information about cultural differences because an inappropriate gesture, reaction, or greeting, even if it is unintentional, might make [15] you an unwelcome guest.

The same gesture can have very different meanings in different countries. The gesture meaning OK in the United States means something completely different in Brazil as Ella [20] Yao discovered. Ella had traveled to Brazil to study and was living with a host family. During dinner, her host asked Ella if she was enjoying the meal. Because her mouth was full of food, Ella gave a signal with her hand that to her meant [25] OK. Although Ella meant the food was good, this symbol in Brazilian culture is extremely rude and her host was deeply offended.

While traveling in Thailand, Elizabeth Brown learned that there are differences in ingredients [30] for food in the United States and Thailand. She stopped at a small, family-owned restaurant in Chiang Mai and ordered spring rolls. She was really enjoying eating them until she got to the last one and noticed that there was an insect [35] inside. She complained to the server. Later, she discovered that although insects are disgusting to most Americans, they are considered a delicacy in some countries.

Formality, especially in business relationships, [40] can also be different from country to country. In the United States, it might be fine to use someone's given name, but in many Asian countries, it is considered rude to use anything but a title and the family name. It might also be [45] common to ask about someone's family during small talk in the United States. Conversely, in some cultures it is considered a taboo, such as in Saudi Arabia, where it is inappropriate to ask about a female you are not related to.

[50] All of these mistakes can be avoided with some research on cultural differences before going abroad. Getting information from websites, talking to people, and watching movies and documentaries set in the country you are visiting [55] are good ways to learn more. However, if you do accidentally offend someone, quickly apologize, and learn from your mistake.

Word Work

7 Complete the sentence with one of the word chunks. Change the tense if necessary.

cultural differences	host family	family-owned restaurant
small talk	learn from my mistake	

a. I want to study abroad in Australia, and I can choose to live with a _____ or live in my own apartment. Which one should I pick?

b. When I first got to Japan, I forgot to take my shoes off when I entered someone's house. I have now _____ and always take them off.

c. When I go to a party, I make _____ with a lot of people. I rarely have long discussions with any of them.

d. There are _____ between Chinese and American societies.

e. I prefer eating in a _____ rather than a fast food place.

Before Reading

1 Quickly skim the email. Look at the title and read the first and the last sentence of each paragraph. What is the purpose of this email?

a. to ask for advice   **b.** to persuade   **c.** to entertain

2 Take one minute to scan the text to identify its organization. Check [✓] the correct box below. Underline any words that support your answer.

☐ block organization   ☐ point by point organization

While Reading

3 As you read the text, annotate it to help you remember significant ideas.

After Reading

4 Associate the email with your personal experiences. Answer the following questions.

a. What would you do in Terra's situation?
b. Do you know anyone who has taken an internship?
c. What was the last difficult decision you had to make?

5 Complete the outline of the text.

a. taking a vacation to Argentina or _____
b. _____
c. _____
d. _____
e. Conclusion: _____

6 Choose the correct ending to complete the statements.

a. According to the email, ...
     i. Terra wants to fly to Argentina on American Airlines.
     ii. Terra can't decide if she should go on vacation or take a job during the summer.
b. When Terra and her friends get full-time jobs ...
     i. they won't have time for vacations together.
     ii. they will have more money to travel.
c. If she takes the internship, Terra ...
     i. will save money by living with her parents.
     ii. will earn a lot of money.

Summer Plans

Hey Cousin,

I hope you don't mind if I ask for your help. I remember that you had a similar problem when you graduated a few years ago. As you know, I graduate in a few months and I can't decide what I should do after graduation. I had originally planned a two-month trip to Argentina, but I just found out that I have been accepted for the internship at American Airlines. Both are great opportunities, but I really need your help in making the right decision.

If I travel to Argentina, I can relax and have fun with my friends. I have never taken a vacation with them and this might be the last time we can all travel together. Once I start working, it will be difficult to take off as much time for a vacation. However, if I take the internship, I might be able to travel with work; I probably won't get any time to relax though. I would have to start the day after graduation and I'll be busy working all the time. It will be very stressful.

Despite the stress, it would be a good career move for me to work for American Airlines. Even though I won't get paid, I would get commercial experience and if I work hard, perhaps they would offer me a job at the end of the summer. This happened to another student last summer. Also, it might look rude to turn down an internship which I applied for and I'll feel bad for wasting their time. But, traveling to Argentina would let me practice my Spanish and I know that most tourism companies want to hire people with good Spanish skills. I also promised my friends that I would go with them. They're counting on me to help share the expenses and I'm afraid that if I don't go, they won't be able to afford it themselves. I really don't want to let them down.

Money is also an issue. Traveling to Argentina will cost a fortune. The airfare is expensive and then there's the cost of accommodation, food, and entertainment. I'll spend all my savings. However, if I take the internship, I won't make any money, but at least I can live at home with my parents and I won't spend any money either.

What would you do? I'd appreciate any advice.

Thanks,

Terra

Word Work

7 | Rewrite the sentences using these word chunks. Change the tense if necessary.

| take off time | be a good career move | cost a fortune | live at home |

a. In the USA, it is not common for children to **stay with their parents** once they've graduated from college.
b. If you get offered an internship as a student, it is difficult to turn down because it will **help your future work**.
c. I would like to **stop working** for awhile and travel around the world, but it **is very expensive**.

Reflection

▶ Which was your favorite text in this unit? Why?

▶ Which reading strategies did you use in this unit?

▶ Which new word chunks will you make an effort to use in the next five days? Choose at least five.

Lessons of Life

Warm Up

Look at the pictures and match the cause (the reason) to the effect (the result).

A   i

B   ii

C   iii

Reading Strategy: Recognizing text organization—cause and effect

Cause and effect texts give reasons and explanations for events, conditions, or behavior. They help us understand why and how things work, or why and how things happen.

For example, "Yong-Ho failed his English test last week because he didn't study for the exam and he always sleeps in English class."

In this example, the **effect** or result is that Yong-Ho failed the English test. The **cause** or reason is that he didn't study or pay attention in class. This is called a cause and effect relationship.

Words and phrases such as "because," "due to (the fact that)," "as a result," "so," "consequently," and "therefore" are used to show cause and effect relationships.

Feedback to Warm Up:
A iii; B i; C ii.

Strategy in Focus

1 What is the cause and effect relationship in this newspaper article? Write the effect and then underline the words that show the cause and effect relationship.

New York Couple Moves to Arizona in Taxi

Like most New Yorkers, Betty and Bob Matas did not need to drive and never learned. This became a problem when they decided to retire to Arizona, over 2,400 miles away. Betty and Bob did not want to frighten their cats by putting them in a plane, so they had to go by car. They couldn't drive, therefore, the couple had to pay $3,000 plus expenses for a five-day taxi ride with their cats to Arizona.

Cause: *They didn't want to frighten their cats in a plane and they couldn't drive.*
Effect: _____

2 What is the cause and effect relationship in this article? Write the effect and then underline the words that show the cause and effect relationship.

How to Become a Millionaire

Making a million dollars is not easy, but almost 10 percent of Americans can call themselves millionaires. The majority of these are ordinary people who share similar attitudes to money. They followed the same basic guidelines to make that first million. Most made their fortune as a result of investing their savings on a regular basis over 20 or more years, consequently earning interest every year and reinvesting it. Also, they are able to invest money because they do not spend more than they earn. Avoiding debt is an important attitude for millionaires. Their simple message is to save money and invest it, and eventually you will become rich. Spending money on lottery tickets is probably not going to make you a millionaire.

a.
Cause: _____
Effect: *Becoming a millionaire*

b.
Cause: *Earning more than spending*
Effect: _____

Feedback:
1. The effect is that Betty and Bob took a taxi to Arizona. The words showing a cause and effect relationship are "so" and "therefore."
2. a. The cause is investing money regularly for a long time.
   b. The effect is being able to invest money.
   The words showing a cause and effect relationship are "as a result," "consequently," and "because."

The Secret to Learning Languages

Before Reading

1 Check [✓] the words that you associate with language learning.

_____ classroom	_____ embarrassed	_____ mistakes
_____ risks	_____ podcasts	_____ movies
_____ grammar	_____ sport clubs	_____ difficult

2 Write any other words you associate with language learning.

_____ _____ _____ _____

3 Look at the title. What do you think the text is about?

While Reading

4 As you read the text, highlight the key ideas in each paragraph.

After Reading

5 Ask a partner the following questions.
   a. Do you behave like a good language learner?
   b. What can you do to become a better language learner?

6 Connect the cause and effect relationships in this text.

Cause		Effect
a. find chances to hear and speak language •	•	**i.** learn language more quickly
b. keep trying to communicate •	•	**ii.** gain a learning opportunity
c. make mistakes •	•	**iii.** learn more of the language

7 Find the underlined words in the text. Deduce the meaning from the context. Then circle the meaning.
   a. An <u>expert</u> is a person who **knows a lot about a subject / is studying a language**.
   b. <u>Behavior</u> is another word for **studying / action**.
   c. An <u>opportunity</u> is a **type of class / chance to do something**.
   d. A <u>laundromat</u> is a place to **wash clothes / draw pictures**.
   e. Being <u>embarrassed</u> is a **positive / negative** feeling.

8 Decide if the statements are true (T) or false (F) according to the text.

a.	**T**	**F**	Learning a new language is impossible for most people.
b.	**T**	**F**	You should learn a language in the classroom.
c.	**T**	**F**	You can learn a language more quickly if you try to use it in your life.
d.	**T**	**F**	It is important that your grammar is perfect to learn a language.
e.	**T**	**F**	Making mistakes is normal and good for language learning.

CD 2:
Track 17

The Secret to Learning Languages

A lot of people think that they are not good at learning a new language. However, experts say that we can all learn from the behavior of good language learners to become better [5] at languages.

Good language learners look for opportunities to hear and use the new language outside of the classroom on a daily basis and consequently learn the language more quickly. If they're [10] studying in a country where the language is spoken, this is easy to do. For instance, they can talk to sales clerks, join sport clubs, or even talk to people in coffee shops. However, if they are studying in a country where the language [15] is not spoken, there are still ways to practice outside of class. They might read newspapers and magazines in that language, watch movies, listen to podcasts, or join chat rooms. All of these are great opportunities to practice and [20] can also be fun.

In addition, good language learners try different ways to make their message understood. For example, if they do not know the word for "laundromat" they might say, "the place where [25] you can wash clothes." If that does not work, they might even try drawing a laundromat with washers and dryers, or acting. The point is that good language learners are creative and do not easily give up. Because of this type of attitude, [30] they learn more than those who get frustrated.

Finally, good language learners are prepared to take risks. They understand that making mistakes is natural and is necessary to learn. As a result, instead of being embarrassed by a [35] mistake or getting frustrated when they do not understand, they see it as gaining a learning opportunity. For example, if they do not understand what someone said the first time, they are not afraid to ask them to repeat it again [40] and again until they do understand. Or, if someone corrects their vocabulary or grammar, they try to remember instead of becoming shy about speaking.

Becoming fluent in a language takes time, it [45] cannot be done in just a few months. However, looking for opportunities to practice the language, trying different ways to communicate, taking risks, and being prepared to make mistakes will help you be a proficient and confident language learner in the long run.

Word Work

9 | **Correct the mistakes in these word chunks.**

   a. When I first started to learn Spanish, I wanted to **give way** because I was ashamed of my accent, and I didn't know any vocabulary.

   b. Even though I am a shy person, I really wanted to learn Spanish so I knew I needed to **make risks** and go to a language club.

   c. I wanted to improve my listening and speaking, so I **entered a Spanish club**.

   d. In my Spanish club, I had to talk with many people, which wasn't always **easy to make**, but I knew it would help to improve my language.

   e. **As a conclusion of** all my hard work, I'm no longer ashamed and I speak Spanish whenever I get the chance.

Cheaters Never Win

Before Reading

1 **What is cheating? Check [✓] your answers.**

a. _____ Helping someone pass a test.   b. _____ Paying someone to do your homework.

c. _____ Asking the teacher for the test questions.   d. _____ Copying answers in a test.

e. _____ Copying from the Internet.   f. _____ Using the same homework again.

2 **Skim the text and decide its main cause and effect idea.**

a. _____ The ways students cheat.

b. _____ The reasons why students cheat.

c. _____ The results of cheating.

While Reading

3 **As you read the text, annotate it to help you remember significant ideas.**

After Reading

4 **Associate the text with your personal experiences. Answer these questions.**

a. Do you know anyone under pressure from their parents to get good grades?

b. Do you have enough time to study?

c. What would happen in your school if a student cheated?

d. Would you be able to use your English in London or New York?

5 **Highlight the key ideas in each paragraph.**

6 **Match the annotation to the paragraph.**

Annotation	Paragraph
Good example of how cheating doesn't help.	1, 2, 3, 4, 5
I can't believe so many have cheated!	1, 2, 3, 4, 5
My friends should follow this advice about copying.	1, 2, 3, 4, 5
She should get a second chance to write the essay.	1, 2, 3, 4, 5

7 **Choose the best ending to the summary.**

The leaflet, *Cheaters Never Win*, helps ...

a. students understand the risks of cheating and gives advice about how to avoid those risks.

b. students with tips to learn French and provides advice to avoid copying their homework from the Internet.

Cheaters Never Win

[1] In a study by the Center for Academic Integrity, 70 percent of students admitted to cheating at least once in their academic career. Students give many reasons for cheating. Some say they are under too much pressure from their parents to get good grades. Others believe it is because they have too little time for studying and homework. Some just do not understand the assignment while a minority blame themselves and their laziness. Whatever the reason, students do not always consider the negative effects of their actions and the severe damage it can cause to their academic and personal life.

[2] First of all, the academic consequences of getting caught. Consider Monica, a college freshman who was taking classes and also working a part time job. She put off doing an essay until the day before it was due. Because she was running out of time, she copied information from a website and handed it in to the teacher. The teacher realized that it was not Monica's work and automatically failed her on that assignment. This is one of the most common disciplinary actions, but students can also fail the class, or even worse, get expelled from school. Is it really worth the risk of ruining your academic career just to save a few hours on some homework?

[3] Not only do students risk their academic career by cheating, but they also prevent themselves from learning. Matt's story fits into this category. He was a high school senior who was having difficulty in his French class. He had friends who were taking the class and were doing really well so he just copied his homework from them. As a result, he did well in the class, but when the class went on a trip to Paris, he had major problems. His friends could talk to storekeepers, order at restaurants, and explore the city without any problems, but he could not say or do anything. By copying his friends' work, Matt never learned French and consequently could not get by easily in Paris.

[4] So, think twice before you copy a friend's homework, buy a research paper from an Internet paper site, or plagiarize even a sentence or two. The consequences of cheating can change your life. Do not be like Monica or Matt—use your time wisely, do your own work and learn more.

[5] If you need extra help or some useful tips on studying, stop by the University Tutoring Center. We have professional tutors who will help you succeed without cheating. The Center is open until midnight, Monday – Friday and no appointment is necessary.

Word Work

8 Make word chunks from the story using the verbs in the box. You may use some of the verbs more than once.

get	put	run	have	think

a. _____ difficulty in

b. _____ off doing

c. _____ twice

d. _____ good grades

e. _____ out of time

f. _____ expelled from school

Reading **3** Dangerous Games

Before Reading

1 **Read the title of the text. What is the purpose of the text?**

  a. To entertain the reader with a story about video gaming.
  b. To persuade parents to stop their children from video gaming.
  c. To inform the reader about the problems caused by video gaming.

While Reading

2 **As you read the text, decide if you want to change your hypothesis.**

3 **Underline statements that confirm your hypothesis.**

After Reading

4 **What is the main cause and effect relationship in this text?**

  a. Computers and videos cause kids to play more video games.
  b. Kids are spending a lot of time gaming and this has a negative effect on their lives.
  c. Playing video games for 16 hours a week causes addiction.

5 **Decide if the statements from the text are fact (F) or opinion (O) according to the writer.**

  a. _____ Childhood is a time of fun and games, ...
  b. _____ A recent survey of children in the United States found that 8- to 12-year-olds spend at least 13 hours a week playing video games ...
  c. _____ One major problem is that kids who spend most of their time gaming might have social and relationship problems.
  d. _____ ... gamers might be out of shape.
  e. _____ ... This happened to a 28-year-old Korean man who spent about 50 hours playing an online video game without sleeping or eating properly.

6 **Check [✓] the inferences you can make about the text.**

  a. _____ Kids got more exercise in the past.
  b. _____ Kids spent more time outside in the past.
  c. _____ Gaming is good for kids.
  d. _____ Parents get upset about low grades.
  e. _____ Kids sleep less today.
  f. _____ Gaming should be banned.

CD 2:
Track 19

Dangerous Games

Childhood is a time of fun and games, and many adults fondly remember their own childhood, playing games like hide-n-seek, tag, and chess. Playing is one way children learn [5] how to interact and get along with others, and it can also be a healthy way to exercise the mind as well as the body. However, play today is not the same. Children today spend most of their play time inside, glued to the computer [10] screen playing video games.

A recent survey of children in the United States found that 8- to 12-year-olds spend at least 13 hours a week playing video games or "gaming" as it is known. Boys in this age group spend [15] even more time, an average of 16 hours a week. Although some will argue that gaming is beneficial because it often involves problem solving, the negative effects are overwhelming.

[20] One major problem is that kids who spend most of their time gaming might have social and relationship problems. Because these kids spend most of their time in isolation interacting with a TV or computer and not with actual [25] people, friendships suffer. They might have trouble sharing, and resolving problems because they do not practice these skills when sitting alone at a computer.

Another potential negative effect that video [30] gaming has is on health. Playing a video game is not a very physical activity and players usually sit in a chair for hours. In addition, players might not take the time to eat a well-balanced meal and will instead snack on whatever is available, [35] whether it is healthy or not. As a result, gamers might be out of shape.

There is also a chance that gamers are more likely to have academic problems because they are spending more time playing their games [40] than working on their homework. This often results in lower grades at school with the unwanted side effect of upsetting parents.

Finally, there is always the possibility that the gamer becomes addicted. It is becoming more [45] common to hear about people who play four or five hours a day or even all day. This happened to a 28-year-old Korean man who spent about 50 hours playing an online video game without sleeping or eating properly. Consequently, his [50] gaming addiction led to his death.

Obviously that is an extreme example of the dangers of video gaming; however, it serves as a reminder that video gaming, like everything else, should be done in moderation. A few [55] hours a week should not hurt, but several hours a day just might be dangerous to your health.

Word Work

7 Circle the correct word chunk.

a. Maya is friendly and **gets along with / gets by with** everyone.

b. I'd rather **buy my time / spend my time** reading than watching television.

c. Ted is a serious gamer; he's **stuck to the computer screen / glued to the computer screen** at all hours of the day.

d. I love eating junk food and I don't like to exercise, so I'm **out of shape / out of size** .

Reflection

▶ Which was your favorite text in this unit? Why?

▶ Which reading strategies did you use in this unit?

▶ Which new word chunks will you make an effort to use in the next five days? Choose at least five.

Review Reading Strategies

- Unit 10: Time order and process
- Unit 11: Compare and contrast
- Unit 12: Cause and effect

1 Read each statement and write the text organization style that is being described.

	Text Organization
a. Gives reasons, explanations, conditions, and behaviors.	
b. Describes how to do something or how something works.	
c. Words used in this text organization include "both," "similar," "same," "also," "alike," "unlike."	
d. Usually tells a story or explains events in the order they happen.	
e. Words used in this text organization include "before," "after," "while," "then," "next," "today."	
f. Describes two similar but different things.	
g. Words used in this text organization include "first," "second," "before," "after," "finally."	

2 Read the first paragraph of the text, *Get Up and Go*. What is the main idea?

a. Regular exercise can lower weight and cholesterol.
b. Exercise is beneficial to neurological and psychological health.
c. Following an exercise program can benefit your mental health.

3 Read the rest of the article and answer the following questions.

a. What is the cause and effect relationship of the second paragraph?
   Cause: increase levels of BDNF's

   Effect: _____

b. What is the cause and effect relationship of the third paragraph?
   Cause: _____

   Effect: improved performance on cognitive tests.

4 Connect the cause and effect relationships in this text.

Cause	Effect
a. sustained level of cerebral blood flow	**i.** general feeling of well-being/acceptance
b. improvement of body shape	**ii.** better performance on memory tests
c. participation in a sports team	**iii.** positive self-image

5 Write down the words in the text used to show cause and effect relationships.

_____ _____ _____ _____ _____

Reading

Get Up and Go

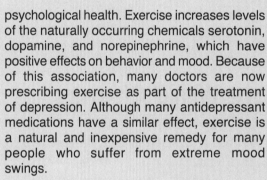

[1] Everyone understands that regular exercise can keep your weight and cholesterol levels down and helps you stay physically fit. However, not many realize the neurological and psychological benefits that following a regular exercise program can have on your health.

[2] Studies show a correlation between exercise and neurological health. Some of these studies examine how regular exercise can both prevent or at least postpone dementia in older adults by increasing the level of brain-derived neurotrophic factors (BDNF). BDNF's main role seems to be in helping brain cells survive longer, therefore ensuring better cognitive functions. Additionally, studies have found that physical activity results in sustained levels of cerebral blood flow and an increase in neural activity in certain parts of the brain that involve attention. This seems to result in older, active adults achieving better results in cognitive memory tests than their sedentary counterparts.

[3] However, it is not only the elderly who can enjoy the neurological benefits of a regular exercise program. Studies involving young adults following a 12-week program of jogging also showed a positive correlation. The group performed significantly better on cognitive tests while exercising compared to when they stopped their running program. Some scientists attribute this to the increased level of oxygen flowing to the brain, a consequence of exercise, which helps in memory formation in young adults.

[4] In addition to these neurological benefits, regular exercise can also improve one's psychological health. Exercise increases levels of the naturally occurring chemicals serotonin, dopamine, and norepinephrine, which have positive effects on behavior and mood. Because of this association, many doctors are now prescribing exercise as part of the treatment of depression. Although many antidepressant medications have a similar effect, exercise is a natural and inexpensive remedy for many people who suffer from extreme mood swings.

[5] Besides boosting these mood-lifting chemicals, exercise can also lead to a greater level of self-esteem. Firstly, exercise usually leads to an improvement of body shape, which results in a more positive self-image. Secondly, individuals who exercise usually have more social interaction, whether they are taking part in a team sport or exercise class, or just seeing others in the gym. As a result, they have a greater feeling of belonging to something, and this can contribute to a general feeling of well-being and acceptance.

[6] With this mounting evidence of the neurological, psychological, and physical attributes of exercise, it is becoming harder to justify sitting on a couch and being glued to a TV or computer screen in your spare time. Following a regular exercise regime will, no doubt, make you physically fitter, but also mentally sharper and emotionally happier.

Comprehension Check

1 The word "correlation" in the passage is closest in meaning to:

   a. opposition.   **b.** benefits.   **c.** connection.   **d.** effects.

2 Which of the following is NOT a benefit of exercise mentioned in the text?

   a. Prevention of dementia.   **b.** Improved memory.
   c. Greater self esteem.   **d.** Less chance of heart disease.

3 In the third paragraph, the word "this" refers to:

   a. neurological benefits.   **b.** a 12-week program of jogging.
   c. better performance on cognitive tests.   **d.** memory formation.

4 In the fifth paragraph, the author mentions joining a sports team as an example of how exercise:

   a. improves your strength.   **b.** improves your body shape.
   c. increases your intelligence.   **d.** increases your social interaction.

5 In the sixth paragraph, the author implies that watching television can be:

   a. unhealthy.   **b.** educational.
   c. entertaining.   **d.** relaxing.

More Word Chunks

1 Match the word chunk from the text with its definition. Then choose one word chunk and write a sentence about yourself or someone you know.

   a. mood swings •   • **i.** confidence
   b. self-esteem •   • **ii.** happiness
   c. self-image •   • **iii.** extreme change in feelings
   d. well-being •   • **iv.** opinion of yourself

2 Complete the text (a promotional leaflet) on the opposite page, using these word chunks from Units 10, 11, and 12.

glued to the computer screen	easy to do	end up in
cost a lot of money	learn from your mistakes	think twice
in just over	out of shape	given up

An Improved You!

Do you feel like you are overweight and (a.) _____ ?

Do you sit on the couch, or sit (b.) _____ every night to help you relax?

Do you feel like you've (c.) _____ on exercising and taking care of yourself?

If you answered yes to any of the questions, then it is time to (d.) _____ ,
join a gym, and start exercising.

Helpful Exercise Tips

Make sure you schedule at least half an hour of exercise into your daily activities. If you do this every
day, (e.) _____ a few months, you'll notice a difference in your health.

Do something fun, like join a sports club or gym. After awhile, you won't even (f.) _____
about exercising because it will be so much fun.

If you don't start taking care of yourself, you might (g.) _____ the
hospital with some weight-related problems and diseases.

So, come on, join Atlas Gym. It's (h.) _____ . You just have to fill out a
short questionnaire and then we'll set up a personalized exercise program. It won't (i.) _____ ,
just $40 a month.

---

3 In Unit 10 we learned about the word chunks "the night before," "work through the night," and "be up all night"

I was up all night working on my research paper. Because I had put off the work for so long and had been partying with my friends **the night before**, I had to **work through the night** in order to finish the paper.

Here are some other word chunks with "night" with their definitions:

in the dead of night (the middle of the night)
have a late night (go to bed late)
a night on the town (to go out and enjoy yourself)
have an early night (to go to bed early)
day and night (all the time without stopping)
a night owl (someone who enjoys staying up late)

Complete the sentences with a word chunk from above.

a. Some people enjoy doing their homework late at night because they are _____ .

b. My flight was leaving at 5 a.m. so I had to _____ .

c. To celebrate my birthday, my friends and I had _____ and went clubbing.

d. Before the exams, I studied _____ in hopes of learning as much as I could.

e. Typically people _____ on New Year's Eve because they are waiting for midnight to arrive.

f. My friend called and woke me up _____ because she wanted to talk about some problems. Although I was really tired, I knew she needed to talk to me, so I wasn't too upset.

Vocabulary Index

UNIT			Page
academic	/ækədɛmɪk/	ADJ Academic means relating to the work done in schools, colleges, and universities, especially work that involves studying and reasoning rather than practical or technical skills.	47
accommodation	/əkɒmədeɪʃən/	N-VAR Accommodations are buildings or rooms where people live or stay.	107
acknowledge	/æknɒlɪdʒ/	V-T If you acknowledge a fact or a situation, you accept or admit that it is true or that it exists. [FORMAL]	41
acquaintance	/əkweɪntəns/	N-COUNT An acquaintance is someone who you have met, but don't know well.	21
addicted	/ədɪktɪd/	ADJ Someone who is addicted to a harmful drug cannot stop taking it.	115
admit	/ædmɪt/	V-T/V-I If you admit that something bad, unpleasant, or embarrassing is true, you agree, often unwillingly, that it is true.	113
adolescent	/ædəlɛsənt/	N-COUNT Adolescent is used to describe young people who are no longer children but who have not yet become adults.	41
after	/æftər/	PREP If you go after someone, you follow or chase them.	59
agent	/eɪdʒənt/	N-COUNT An agent is a person who arranges work or business for someone else or does business on their behalf. [BUSINESS]	11
agricultural	/ægrɪkʌltʃərəl/	ADJ Agricultural means involving or relating to farming crops and animals.	69
airfare	/ɛərfɛər/	N-COUNT The airfare to a place is the amount it costs to fly there.	107
allergic	/əlɜrdʒɪk/	ADJ If you have an allergic reaction to something, you become ill or get a rash when you eat it, smell it, or touch it.	79
analytic	/ænəlɪtɪk/	ADJ An analytic way of doing something involves the use of logical reasoning.	39
ancient	/eɪnʃənt/	ADJ Ancient means very old, or having existed for a long time.	67
anesthetic	/ænɪsθɛtɪk/	N-MASS Anesthetic is a substance doctors use to stop you feeling pain during an operation, either in the whole of your body when you are unconscious (general anesthetic), or in a part of your body when you are awake (local anesthetic).	75
anxious	/æŋkʃəs/	ADJ If you are anxious, you are nervous or worried about something.	13
apologize	/əpɒlədʒaɪz/	V-I When you apologize to someone, you say that you are sorry that you have hurt them or caused trouble for them. You can say "I apologize" as a formal or polite way of saying sorry.	15
apply for	/əplaɪ fər/	V-T/V-I If you apply for something such as a job or membership of an organization, you write a letter or fill out a form in order to ask formally for it.	107
appointment	/əpɔɪntmənt/	N-COUNT If you have an appointment with someone, you have arranged to see them at a particular time, usually in connection with their work or for a serious purpose.	113
approach	/əproʊtʃ/	N-COUNT Your approach to a task, problem, or situation is the way you deal with it or think about it.	83
articulate	/ɑrtɪkyəlɪt/	ADJ If you describe someone as articulate, you mean that they are able to express their thoughts and ideas easily and well.	43
assassinate	/əsæsɪneɪt/	V-T When someone important is assassinated, they are murdered as a political act.	11
asthma	/æzmə/	N-UNCOUNT Asthma is a lung condition that causes difficulty in breathing.	79
attack	/ətæk/	N-COUNT An attack of an illness is a short period in which you suffer badly from it.	79
bandage	/bændɪdʒ/	V-T If you bandage a wound or part of someone's body, you tie a bandage around it.	15

basis	/beɪsɪs/	N-SING If something is done on a particular basis, it is done according to that method, system, or principle.	111
beneficial	/bɛnɪfɪʃəl/	ADJ Something that is beneficial helps people or improves their lives.	115
Bible	/baɪbəl/	N-PROPER The Bible is the sacred book of the Christian and Jewish religion.	49
bilingual	/baɪlɪŋgwəl/	ADJ Someone who is bilingual can speak two languages equally well.	11
biological	/baɪəlɒdʒɪkəl/	ADJ Biological is used to describe processes and states that occur in the bodies and cells of living things.	41
blame	/bleɪm/	V-T If you blame a person or thing for something bad, or if you blame something bad on somebody, you believe or say that they are responsible for it or that they caused it.	113
broke	/broʊk/	ADJ If you are broke, you have no money. [INFORMAL]	17
champion	/tʃæmpiən/	N-COUNT A champion is someone who has won the first prize in a competition.	71
chant	/tʃænt/	N-COUNT A chant is a religious song or prayer that is sung on only a few notes.	67
chat room	/tʃæt rum/	N-COUNT A chat room is a site on the Internet where people can exchange messages about a particular subject. [COMPUTING]	111
check	/tʃɛk/	N-COUNT A check is a printed form on which you write an amount of money and who it is to be paid to. Your bank then pays the money to that person from your account.	51
checkup	/tʃɛkʌp/	N-COUNT A checkup is a medical examination by a doctor or a dentist to make sure that there is nothing wrong with your health.	79
civil war	/sɪvəl wɔr/	N-COUNT A civil war is a war which is fought between different groups of people who live in the same country.	19
coed	/koʊɛd/	ADJ A coed (coeducational) school, college, or university is attended by both girls and boys.	41
colleague	/kɒlig/	N-COUNT Your colleagues are the people you work with, especially in a professional job.	13
commercial	/kəmɜrʃəl/	ADJ Commercial organizations and activities are concerned with making profits.	47
commit	/kəmɪt/	V-T/V-I If you commit yourself to something, you accept it fully or say that you will definitely do it.	43
common	/kɒmən/	ADJ If something is common, it is found in large numbers or it happens often.	13
companion	/kəmpænyən/	N-COUNT A companion is someone who you spend time with or who you are traveling with.	15
confidence	/kɒnfɪdəns/	N-UNCOUNT If you have confidence, you feel sure about your abilities, qualities, or ideas.	13
conflict	/kɒnflɪkt/	N-VAR Conflict is fighting between countries or groups of people. [WRITTEN]	69
context	/kɒntɛkst/	N-VAR The context of an idea or event is the general situation in which it occurs.	39
conversely	/kɒnvɜrsli, kən/	ADV You say conversely to indicate that the situation you are about to describe is the opposite or reverse of the one you have just described. [FORMAL]	39
coordination	/koʊɔrdəneɪʃən/	N-UNCOUNT Coordination is the ability to use the different parts of your body together efficiently.	41
cop	/kɒp/	N-COUNT A cop is a policeman or policewoman. [INFORMAL]	59
corpse	/kɔrps/	N-COUNT A corpse is a dead body.	11
count on	/kaʊnt ɒn/	PHRASAL VERB If you count on someone or something, you rely on them to support you.	107
counter	/kaʊntər/	N-COUNT In a store or café, a counter is a long flat surface at which customers are served.	23
countless	/kaʊntlɪs/	ADJ Countless means very many.	47

court	/kɔrt/	N-COUNT A court is a place where legal matters are decided by a judge and jury or by a magistrate.	103
critic	/krɪtɪk/	N-COUNT A critic is a person who writes about and expresses opinions about books, movies, music, or art.	27
criticism	/krɪtɪsɪzəm/	N-VAR Criticism is the action of expressing disapproval of something or someone. A criticism is a statement that expresses disapproval.	11
deadline	/dɛdlaɪn/	N-COUNT A deadline is a time or date before which a particular task must be finished or a particular thing must be done.	13
deck	/dɛk/	N-COUNT The deck of a ship is the top part of it that forms a floor in the open air which you can walk on.	19
defect	/difɛkt /	N-COUNT A defect is a fault or imperfection in a person or thing.	83
delicacy	/dɛlɪkəsi/	N-COUNT A delicacy is a rare or expensive food that is considered especially nice to eat.	105
democracy	/dɪmɒkrəsɪ/	N-UNCOUNT Democracy is a system of government in which people choose their rulers by voting for them in elections.	69
demon	/dimən/	N-COUNT A demon is an evil spirit.	31
depression	/dɪprɛʃən/	N-VAR Depression is a mental state in which you are sad and feel that you cannot enjoy anything.	85
desperate	/dɛspərɪt/	ADJ If you are desperate, you are in such a bad situation that you are willing to try anything to change it.	27
despite	/dɪspaɪt/	PREP You use despite to introduce a fact which makes something surprising.	13
destined	/dɛstɪnd/	ADJ If something is destined to happen or if someone is destined to behave in a particular way, that thing seems certain to happen or be done.	43
device	/dɪvaɪs/	N-COUNT A device is an object that has been invented for a particular purpose, for example, for recording or measuring something.	77
diligent	/dɪlɪdʒənt/	ADJ Someone who is diligent works hard in a careful and thorough way.	47
disgusting	/dɪsɡʌstɪŋ/	ADJ If you say that something is disgusting, you think it is extremely unpleasant or unacceptable.	105
doubt	/noʊ daʊt/	PHRASE You use no doubt to emphasize that something seems certain or very likely to you.	11
draft	/dræft/	N-COUNT A draft is an early version of a letter, book, or speech.	13
drop	/drɒp/	V-T If you drop an idea, course of action, or habit, you do not continue with it.	79
election	/ɪlɛkʃən/	N-VAR An election is a process in which people vote to choose a person or group of people to hold an official position.	69
eliminate	/ɪlɪmɪneɪt/	V-T To eliminate something means to remove it completely. [FORMAL]	69
encourage	/ɪnkɜrɪdʒ/	V-T If you encourage someone, you give them confidence, for example by letting them know that what they are doing is good.	57
endurance	/ɪndʊrəns/	N-UNCOUNT Endurance is the ability to continue with an unpleasant or difficult situation, experience, or activity over a long period of time.	67
enlightenment	/ɪnlaɪtənmənt/	N-UNCOUNT In Buddhism, enlightenment is a final spiritual state in which everything is understood and there is no more suffering or desire.	67
evidence	/ɛvɪdəns/	N-UNCOUNT Evidence is anything that makes you believe that something is true or has really happened.	103
evolution	/ivəluʃən/	N-UNCOUNT Evolution is a process of gradual change that takes place over many generations, during which species of animals, plants, or insects slowly change some of their physical characteristics.	83
except	/ɪksɛpt/	CONJ You use except or except for to introduce the only thing or person that a statement does not apply to, or a fact that prevents a statement from being completely true.	31

exhausting	/ɪgzɔstɪŋ/	ADJ If something is exhausting, it makes you so tired, either physically or mentally, that you have no energy left.	15
exotic	/ɪgzɒtɪk/	ADJ Something that is exotic is unusual and interesting, usually because it comes from or is related to a distant country.	15
expense	/ɪkspɛns/	N-VAR Expense is the money that something costs you or that you need to spend in order to do something.	107
extracurricular	/ɛkstrəkərɪkyʊlər/	ADJ Extracurricular activities are activities for students that are not part of their course. [FORMAL]	13
fluent	/fluənt/	ADJ Someone who is fluent in a particular language can speak the language easily and correctly. You can also say that someone speaks fluent French, Chinese, or some other language.	111
fondly	/fɒndli/	ADV You use fondly to describe people or their behavior when they show affection.	115
formula	/fɔrmyələ/	N-COUNT A formula is a group of letters, numbers, or other symbols which represents a scientific or mathematical rule.	21
fortune	/fɔrtʃən/	N-COUNT Someone who has a fortune has a very large amount of money.	15
fountain	/faʊntɪn/	N-COUNT A fountain is an ornamental feature in a pool or lake which consists of a jet of water that is forced up into the air by a pump.	15
fume	/fyum/	V-T If you fume over something, you express annoyance and anger about it.	57
funeral	/fyunərəl/	N-COUNT A funeral is the ceremony that is held when the body of someone who has died is buried or cremated.	11
gain	/geɪn/	V-T If you gain something, you obtain it, usually after a lot of effort.	57
goose bumps	/gus bʌmps/	N-PLURAL If you get goose bumps, the hairs on your skin stand up so that it is covered with tiny bumps. You get goose bumps when you are cold, frightened, or excited.	23
guideline	/gaɪdlaɪn/	N-COUNT If an organization issues guidelines on something, it issues official advice about how to do it.	55
hideous	/hɪdiəs/	ADJ If you say that someone or something is hideous, you mean that they are very ugly or unpleasant.	31
human rights	/hyumən raɪts/	N-PLURAL Human rights are basic rights which many societies believe that all people should have.	69
hysterically	/hɪstɛrɪkəli/	ADV Laughing hysterically means laughing in a loud and uncontrolled manner. [INFORMAL]	87
immense	/ɪmɛns/	ADJ If you describe something as immense, you mean that it is extremely large or great.	19
immigrants	/ɪmɪgrənt/	N-COUNT An immigrant is a person who has come to live in a country from some other country. Compare emigrant.	29
impatient	/ɪmpeɪʃənt/	ADJ If you are impatient to do something or impatient for something to happen, you are eager to do it or for it to happen and do not want to wait.	51
in isolation	/ɪn aɪsəleɪʃən/	PHRASE If someone does something in isolation, they do it without other people present or without their help.	115
in the long run	/ɪn ðə lɒŋ rʌn/	PHRASE If you talk about what will happen in the long run, you are saying what you think will happen over a long period of time in the future.	111
inanimate	/ɪnænɪmɪt/	ADJ An inanimate object is one that has no life.	39
inappropriate	/ɪnəproʊpriɪt/	ADJ Something that is inappropriate is not suitable for a particular situation or purpose.	55
incident	/ɪnsɪdənt/	N-COUNT An incident is something that happens, often something that is unpleasant. [FORMAL]	19
inconvenience	/ɪnkənviniəns/	V-T If someone inconveniences you, they cause problems or difficulties for you.	55
insist	/ɪnsɪst/	V-T/V-I If you insist that something is true, you say so very firmly and refuse to change your mind.	49

integrity	/ɪntɛgrɪti/	N-UNCOUNT If you have integrity, you are honest and firm in your moral principles.	113
internship	/ɪntɜrnʃɪp/	N-COUNT An internship is the position held by an advanced student or a recent graduate, especially in medicine, who is being given practical training under supervision. (AM)	27
intervene	/ɪntərvin/	N-VAR If you intervene in a situation, you become involved in it and try to change it.	71
invent	/ɪnvɛnt/	V-T If you invent something such as a machine or process, you are the first person to think of it or make it.	77
irritated	/ɪrɪteɪtəd/	ADJ If you are irritated, you are annoyed about something.	57
jail	/dzeɪl/	N-VAR A jail is a place where criminals are kept in order to punish them.	15
journalist	/dʒɜrnəlɪst/	N-COUNT A journalist is a person whose job is to collect news and write about it for newspapers, magazines, television, or radio.	11
kidnap	/kɪdnæp/	V-T To kidnap someone is to take them away illegally and by force, and usually to hold them prisoner in order to demand something from their family, employer, or government.	31
let down	/lɛt daʊn/	PHRASAL VERB If you let someone down, you disappoint them, by not doing something that you have said you will do or that they expected you to do.	107
linguistics	/lɪŋwɪstɪks/	N-PLURAL Linguistics is the study of the way in which language works.	57
mask	/mæsk/	N-COUNT A mask is something which you wear over your face for protection or to disguise yourself.	59
mathematician	/mæθəmætɪʃən/	N-COUNT A mathematician is a person who is trained in the study of mathematics.	21
memoirs	/mɛmwɑrz/	N-PLURAL A person's memoirs are a written account of the people who they have known and events that they remember.	29
micro-chip	/maɪkroʊtʃɪp/	N-COUNT A microchip is a very small piece of silicon inside a computer. It has electronic circuits on it and can hold large quantities of information or perform mathematical or logical operations.	77
minority	/mɪnɔrɪti, maɪ–/	N-SING If you talk about a minority of people or things in a larger group, you are referring to a number of them that forms less than half of the larger group, usually much less than half.	113
miracle	/mɪrəkəl/	N-COUNT A miracle is a wonderful and surprising event that is believed to be caused by God.	49
moderation	/mɒdəreɪʃən/	N-UNCOUNT If you say that someone's behavior shows moderation, you approve of them because they act in a way that is reasonable and not extreme.	115
mosque	/mɔsk/	N-COUNT A mosque is a building where Muslims go to worship.	15
nagging	/næggɪŋ/	ADJ A nagging pain is not very severe but is difficult to cure.	79
natural	/nætʃərəl/	ADJ Someone with a natural ability or skill was born with that ability and did not have to learn it.	47
nausea	/nɔrziə, –ʒə, –siə, ʃə/	N-UNCOUNT Nausea is a feeling that you are going to vomit.	75
navigational	/nævɪgeɪʃənəl/	ADJ Navigational means relating to the act of moving a ship or an aircraft.	49
no wonder	/noʊ wʌndər/	PHRASE If you say "no wonder," "little wonder," or "small wonder," you mean that something is not surprising.	57
odds	/ɒdz/	N-PLURAL You refer to how likely something is to happen as the odds that it will happen.	21
offend	/əfɛnd/	V-T/V-I If you offend someone, you say or do something which upsets or embarrasses them.	105
old	/oʊld/	ADJ You use old to refer to something that used to belong to you, or to a person or thing that used to have a particular role in your life.	41
operator	/ɒpəreɪtər/	N-COUNT An operator is a person who connects telephone calls at a telephone exchange or in a place such as an office or hotel.	87
ordinary	/ɔrdənɛri/	ADJ Ordinary people or things are normal and not special or different in any way.	83

originally	/ərɪdʒɪnəli/	ADV When you say what happened or was the case originally, you are saying what happened or was the case when something began or came into existence, often to contrast it with what happened later.	23
outline	/aʊtlaɪn/	N-COUNT An outline is a general explanation or description of something.	13
overtime	/oʊvərtaɪm/	N-UNCOUNT Overtime is time that you spend doing your job in addition to your normal working hours.	43
overwhelmed	/oʊvərwɛlmd/	ADJ If you are overwhelmed by a feeling or event, it affects you very strongly, and you do not know how to deal with it.	85
packed	/pækt/	ADJ A place that is packed is very crowded.	51
paper	/peɪpər/	N-COUNT A paper is a long piece of writing on an academic subject.	77
perseverance	/pɜrsɪvɪərəns/	N-UNCOUNT Perseverance is the quality of continuing with something even though it is difficult.	71
persuade	/pərsweɪd/	V-T If you persuade someone to do something, you cause them to do it by giving them good reasons for doing it.	23
plagiarize	/pleɪdʒəraɪz/	V-T If someone plagiarizes another person's idea or work, they use it or copy it and pretend that they thought of it or created it.	113
podcast	/pɒdkæst/	N-COUNT A podcast is an audio file similar to a radio broadcast, that can be downloaded and listened to on a computer or MP3 player.	111
pop	/pɒp/	V-T If you pop something somewhere, you put it there quickly. [INFORMAL]	87
poverty	/pɒvərti/	N-UNCOUNT Poverty is the state of being very poor.	27
prank	/præŋk/	N-COUNT A prank is a childish trick.	87
precaution	/prɪkɔʃən/	N-COUNT A precaution is an action that is intended to prevent something dangerous or unpleasant from happening.	87
probability	/prɒbəbɪlɪti/	N-VAR The probability of something happening is how likely it is to happen.	21
procrastination	/proʊkræstɪneɪʃən/	N-UNCOUNT Procrastination means leaving things you should do until later, often because you do not want to do them.	13
professional	/prəfɛʃənəl/	N-COUNT Professionals are people whose jobs require special training.	85
proficient	/prəfɪʃənt/	ADJ If you are proficient in something, you can do it well.	111
promptly	/prɒmptli/	ADV If you do something promptly, you do it immediately.	15
psychologist	/saɪkɒlədʒist/	N-COUNT A psychologist is a person who studies the human mind and tries to explain why people behave in the way that they do.	39
publish	/pʌblɪʃ/	V-T When a company publishes a book or magazine, it prints copies of it, which are sent to stores to be sold.	39
quadriplegic	/kwɒdrɪplidʒɪk/	N-COUNT A quadriplegic is a person who is permanently unable to use their arms and legs.	77
rebel	/rɛbəl/	N-COUNT Rebels are people who are fighting against their own country's army in order to change the political system there.	29
referee	/rɛfəri/	N-COUNT The referee is the official who controls a sports event such as a football game or a boxing match.	71
reflect	/rɪflɛkt/	V-T If something reflects an attitude or situation, it shows that the attitude or situation exists.	13
refugee	/rɛfyudʒi/	N-COUNT Refugees are people who have been forced to leave their homes or their country, either because there is a war there or because of their political or religious beliefs.	29
related	/rɪleɪtɪd/	ADJ People who are related belong to the same family.	17
release	/rɪlis/	V-T If a person or animal is released, they are set free.	103
remind	/rɪmaɪnd/	V-T If you say that someone or something reminds you of another person or thing, you mean that they are similar to the other person or thing and that they make you think about them.	23
reminder	/rɪmaɪndər/	N-COUNT Something that serves as a reminder of another thing makes you think about the other thing.	115

revenge	/rɪvɛndʒ/	N-UNCOUNT Revenge involves hurting or punishing someone who has hurt or harmed you.	103
ritual	/rɪtʃuəl/	N-VAR A ritual is a religious service or other ceremony which involves a series of actions performed in a fixed order.	67
robber	/rɒbər/	N-COUNT A robber is someone who steals money or property from a bank, store, or vehicle, often by using force or threats.	15
round	/raʊnd/	N-COUNT In a boxing or wrestling match, a round is one of the periods during which the boxers or wrestlers fight.	71
schedule	/skɛdʒul, –uəl/	N-COUNT A schedule is a plan that gives a list of events or tasks and the times at which each one should happen or be done.	13
science fiction	/saɪəns fɪkʃən/	N-UNCOUNT Science fiction (sci-fi) consists of stories in books, magazines, and movies about events that take place in the future or in other parts of the universe.	77
self-awareness	/sɛlf əwɛərnɛs/	N-UNCOUNT Someone who has self-awareness knows and judges their own character well.	85
sentence	/sɛntəns/	V-T When a judge sentences someone, he or she states in court what their punishment will be.	103
settle	/sɛtl/	V-T/V-I If you settle yourself somewhere or settle somewhere, you sit down or make yourself comfortable.	87
severe	/sɪvɪər/	ADJ You use severe to indicate that something bad or undesirable is great or intense.	11
shore	/ʃɔr/	N-COUNT The shores or shore of an ocean or lake is the land along the edge of it.	19
side effect	/saɪd ɪfɛkt/	N-COUNT The side effects of a drug are the effects, usually bad ones, that the drug has on you in addition to its function of curing illness or pain.	75
significance	/sɪgnɪfɪkəns/	N-UNCOUNT The significance of something is the importance that it has.	23
siren	/saɪrən/	N-COUNT A siren is a warning device which makes a long, loud noise. Most fire engines, ambulances, and police cars have sirens.	59
slang	/slæŋ/	N-UNCOUNT Slang consists of words, expressions, and meanings that are very informal and are used by people who know each other very well or who have the same interests.	55
slavery	/sleɪvəri/	N-UNCOUNT Slavery is the system by which people are owned by other people as slaves.	11
smuggling	/smʌgəl ɪŋ/	ADJ If someone is involved in a smuggling operation, they take things or people into a place or out of it, illegally or secretly.	49
snack	/snæk/	V-I If you snack, you eat snacks between meals.	115
socialize	/soʊʃəlaɪz/	V-I If you socialize, you meet other people socially, for example at parties.	47
sophisticated	/səfɪstɪkeɪtɪd/	ADJ Someone who is sophisticated is comfortable in social situations and knows about culture, fashion, and other matters that are considered socially important.	43
stained	/steɪnd/	ADJ If something is stained, there is a mark that is difficult to remove.	51
stand up to	/stænd ʌp tu/	PHRASAL VERB If you stand up to someone more powerful than you, you defend yourself against their attacks or demands.	31
starvation	/stɑrveɪʃən/	N-UNCOUNT Starvation is extreme suffering or death, caused by lack of food.	49
stockbroker	/stɒkbroʊkər/	N-COUNT A stockbroker is a person whose job is to buy and sell stocks and shares for people who want to invest money. [BUSINESS]	27
storm out of	/stɔrm oʊt ɒv/	PHRASAL VERB If you storm into or out of a place, you enter or leave it quickly and noisily, because you are angry.	51
strained	/streɪnd/	ADJ If relations between people are strained, those people do not like or trust each other.	51
strand	/strænd/	V-T If you are stranded, you are prevented from leaving a place, for example because of bad weather.	19

subconscious	/sʌbkɒnʃəs/	N-SING Your subconscious is the part of your mind that can influence you or affect your behavior even though you are not aware of it.	75
superstition	/supərstɪʃən/	N-VAR Superstition is belief in things that are not real or possible, for example magic.	15
surgery	/sɜrdʒəri/	N-UNCOUNT Surgery is medical treatment in which your body is cut open so that a doctor can repair, remove, or replace a diseased or damaged part.	75
syllabus	/sɪləbəs/	N-COUNT A syllabus is an outline or summary of the subjects to be covered in a course.	55
taboo	/tæbu/	N-COUNT A taboo against a subject or activity is a social custom to avoid doing that activity or talking about that subject, because people find it embarrassing or offensive.	105
technique	/tɛknik/	N-COUNT A technique is a particular method of doing an activity, usually a method that involves practical skills.	85
theory	/θɪəri/	N-VAR A theory is a formal idea or set of ideas intended to explain something and which is capable of being tested.	21
therapy	/θɛrəpi/	N-VAR Therapy or a therapy is a treatment for a particular illness or condition. [MEDICAL]	83
third world	/θɜrd wɜrld/	ADJ Countries that are poor and do not have much industrial development are sometimes referred to together as third world. Some people find this term offensive.	29
to death	/tu dɛθ/	PHRASE You use to death after an adjective or a verb to emphasize the action, state, or feeling mentioned. For example, if you are frightened to death or bored to death, you are extremely frightened or bored.	59
tournament	/tʊərnəmənt/	N-COUNT A tournament is a sports competition in which players who win a game continue to play further game in the competition until just one person or team is left.	71
transfer	/trænsfɛr /	V-T/V-I If you are transferred, or if you transfer, to a different job or place, you move to a different job or place within the same organization.	43
trauma	/traʊmə, trɔ-/	N-VAR Trauma is a very severe shock or very upsetting experience, which may cause psychological damage.	83
unconscious	/ʌnkɒnʃəs/	ADJ Someone who is unconscious is in a state similar to sleep, usually as the result of a serious injury or a lack of oxygen.	75
unwelcome	/ʌnwɛlkəm/	ADJ If you say that a visitor is unwelcome, you mean that you did not want them to come.	105
unwitting	/ʌnwɪtɪŋ/	ADJ A person does an unwitting action without realizing it.	59
urgent	/ɜrdʒənt/	ADJ If something is urgent, it needs to be dealt with as soon as possible.	55
vegetarian	/vɛdʒɪtɛəriən/	N-COUNT Someone who is vegetarian never eats meat or fish.	67
warrior	/wɒriər/	N-COUNT A warrior is a fighter or soldier, especially one in former times who was very brave and experienced in fighting.	31
withdrawal	/wɪðdrɔəl, -wɪθ/	N-COUNT A withdrawal is an amount of money that you take from your bank account.	59
witness	/wɪtnɪs/	N-COUNT A witness to an event such as an accident or crime is a person who saw it.	103
wizard	/wɪzərd/	N-COUNT In legends and fairy tales, a wizard is a man who has magic powers.	11
work out	/wɜrk aʊt/	PHRASAL VERB If a situation works out well or works out, it happens or progresses in a satisfactory way.	11
workshop	/wɜrkʃɒp/	N-COUNT A workshop is a period of discussion or practical work on a particular subject in which a group of people share their knowledge or experience.	85
yacht	/yɒt/	N-COUNT A yacht is a large boat with sails or a motor, used for racing or pleasure trips.	19

Reading Strategies Index

Unit 1
Reading 1: Skimming (2); Scanning (3)
Reading 2: Skimming (2); Scanning (3); Recognizing main ideas (6)
Reading 3: Skimming (1); Scanning (1, 3)

Unit 2
Reading 1: Making predictions (2, 3); Making inferences (4); Deducing (5)
Reading 2: Skimming (1); Interpreting (3); Deducing (4)
Reading 3: Making predictions (3); Making inferences (5)

Unit 3
Reading 1: Skimming (1); Making judgments (2, 3); Visualizing (4); Making associations (5); Summarizing (6)
Reading 2: Making associations (1); Visualizing (2, 3); Making judgments (4); Summarizing (5)
Reading 3: Making associations (1, 4); Visualizing (2, 3); Summarizing (5)

Review 1
Reading Strategies Review: Skimming (2); Scanning (3); Making inferences (4)
Comprehension Check: Deducing meaning of words from context (2, 4); Scanning (3); Summarizing (5)

Unit 4
Reading 1: Skimming (1); Understanding tone (1, 4); Understanding purpose (3, 4); Making judgments (5); Making inferences (6)
Reading 2: Understanding purpose (1); Understanding tone (4); Making judgments (5)
Reading 3: Skimming (1) ; Understanding tone (1, 3, 4, 5); Understanding purpose (2, 3); Making judgments (4); Interpreting (6)

Unit 5
Reading 1: Scanning (2); Making judgments (3, 4); Separating fact from opinion (5, 6);
Reading 2: Skimming (1); Separating fact from opinion (2); Making judgments (3); Making associations (5); Making inferences (6)
Reading 3: Making predictions (2, 3); Separating fact from opinion (5); Making judgments (4)

Unit 6
Reading 1: Skimming (2); Interpreting (3); Making judgments (4); Referencing (5)
Reading 2: Making judgments (1); Skimming (2); Making associations (4); Referencing (5)
Reading 3: Visualize (2, 3); Making inferences (4); Referencing (5)

Review 2
Reading Strategies Review: Understanding purpose (2, 3); Understanding tone (4); Separating fact from opinion (5); Referencing (6)
Comprehension Check: Deducing meaning of words from context (1); Inferring (2, 5); Scanning (3, 4)

Unit 7
Reading 1: Skimming (2); Highlighting (4); Annotating (4); Summarizing (6)
Reading 2: Annotate (3, 4); Highlighting (5)
Reading 3: Making associations (2); Visualizing (3, 5); Highlighting (4); Annotating (4); Making judgments (6)

Unit 8
Reading 1: Skimming (1); Recognizing main ideas (1–5); Highlighting (4, 5); Making judgments (3); Referencing (6)
Reading 2: Skimming (2); Recognizing main ideas (2, 5); Visualizing (3, 4)
Reading 3: Understanding purpose (1); Recognizing main ideas (2, 4); Making judgments (3)

Unit 9
Reading 1: Making associations (1, 4); Skimming (2); Recognizing main ideas (2, 5, 6, 7); Highlighting (5, 6, 7); Recognizing supporting ideas (5, 6)
Reading 2: Skimming (1); Recognizing main ideas (1, 3, 5); Annotating (2); Highlighting (3, 5); Recognizing supporting ideas (4, 6); Separating fact from opinion (7)
Reading 3: Recognizing main ideas (2); Making judgments (3); Deducing (4)

Review 3
Reading Strategies Review: Recognizing main ideas (2); Highlighting (3); Annotating (4); Recognizing supporting ideas (5)
Comprehension Check: Deducing meaning of words from context (1, 2); Referencing (4); Scanning (3, 5)

Unit 10
Reading 1: Time order and process (1, 6); Scanning (1); Skimming (2); Recognizing main ideas (2); Making predictions (3, 4); Deducing (7)
Reading 2: Skimming (1); Recognizing main ideas (1); Scanning (2); Time order and process (2); Making judgments (3, 4); Summarizing (6)
Reading 3: Scanning (1); Time order and process (1, 5); Recognizing main ideas (2); Referencing (4)

Unit 11
Reading 1: Skimming (1); Recognizing main ideas (1); Compare and Contrast (2, 4); Making judgments (3)
Reading 2: Skimming (1); Recognizing main ideas (1); Scanning (2); Visualizing (3, 4); Compare and Contrast (5); Making inferences (6)
Reading 3: Understanding purpose (1); Recognizing main ideas (1); Scanning (2); Annotating (3); Making associations (4); Compare and Contrast (5)

Unit 12
Reading 1: Making associations (1, 2); Recognizing main ideas (3); Highlighting (4); Making judgments (5); Cause and effect (6); Deducing (7)
Reading 2: Skimming (2); Cause and effect (2); Annotating (3); Making associations (4); Highlighting (5); Annotating (6); Summarizing (7)
Reading 3: Skimming (1); Understanding purpose (1); Recognizing main ideas (1–3); Cause and effect (4); Separating fact from opinion (5); Making inferences (6)

Review 4
Reading Strategies Review: Recognizing main ideas (2); Cause and effect (3–5)
Comprehension Check: Deducing meaning of words from context (1); Scanning (2, 4, 5); Referencing (3)